The Originality of *Madame Bovary*

Le Romantisme et après en France
Romanticism and after in France

Volume 6

Edited by Alan Raitt

Peter Lang

Oxford · Bern · Berlin · Bruxelles · Frankfurt am Main · New York · Wien

Alan Raitt

The Originality
of *Madame Bovary*

Peter Lang

Oxford·Bern·Berlin·Bruxelles·Frankfurt am Main·New York·Wien

Die Deutsche Bibliothek – CIP-Einheitsaufnahme

Raitt, Alan:
The originality of Madame Bovary / Alan Raitt. – Oxford ; Bern ; Berlin ;
Bruxelles ; Frankfurt am Main ; New York ; Wien : Lang, 2002
(Romanticism and after in France ; Vol. 6)
ISBN 3-906768-44-9

ISSN 1422-4896
ISBN 3-906768-44-9
US-ISBN 0-8204-5856-2

© Peter Lang AG, European Academic Publishers, Bern 2002
Jupiterstrasse 15, Postfach, 3000 Bern 15, Switzerland
info@peterlang.com, www.peterlang.com, www.peterlang.net

Printed in Germany

Table of contents

Acknowledgements

My first debt of gratitude is to my friend and colleague Dr Adrianne Tooke of Somerville College, Oxford, who kindly read a draft of this book and made many invaluable suggestions for improvements, though of course any shortcomings are solely my responsibility. I have also derived much benefit and encouragement from regular conversations on Flaubert with Dr Anthony Pilkington of Jesus College, Oxford. I am profoundly grateful to my wife, Lia, and to Professors Mike Freeman and Tim Unwin for undertaking the daunting task of converting my incompetent typescript into something publishable. My thanks are due to Dr Graham Speake for his support and forbearance on behalf of Peter Lang.

Preface

Julian Barnes, who makes no secret of his near-fetishistic pre-occupation with Flaubert, recently asked: 'Why is *Madame Bovary* the first modern novel?', adding that there are many different (and conclusive) answers to the question.[1] The purpose of this book is to suggest some of them, by trying to see what features of *Madame Bovary* represent new departures in the evolution of the novel generally. It is of course posssible to argue that *Madame Bovary* may have less claim to be considered the first modern novel than *L'Education sentimentale*. Marion Schmid has for instance declared that *L'Education sentimentale* is 'commonly considered Flaubert's masterpiece and the first prototype of the modern novel'.[2] It may well be that the later novel is even more radical in its break with previous practice than *Madame Bovary*, but that does not alter the fact that Flaubert's first published novel is extraordinarily innovative and that all kinds of development in the nineteenth- and twentieth-century novel can be traced back to its example.

That is not to say that the aim of this study is to define the impact made by *Madame Bovary* on subsequent novel-writing, which would entail examining the work of many authors operating after its publication, including the Goncourt brothers, Huysmans, Zola, Maupassant, Theodor Fontane, Galdós, Eça de Queirós, Henry James, Joyce, Proust, Nabokov, Perec, Vargos Llosa, the *nouveaux romanciers* and many others. This fascinating topic has already received treatment in numerous articles devoted to the debt owed to Flaubert by individual writers, and in more general if summary terms by various critics and literary historians such as Claude Mouchard and Jacques Neefs,[3] Nathalie Sarraute,[4] Stephen Heath[5] and Mireille Naturel,[6] to name only a few.

My objective is rather to see in what ways Flaubert produced in *Madame Bovary* innovations of intention, style and structure and to what extent that novel differed from anything written by previous novelists, most notably Balzac, usually regarded as his closest predecessor. A glance at my chapter-headings immediately reveals that many of the subjects covered would have to be treated at book length if they were to be analysed exhaustively – and indeed book-length treatments of a number of them already exist (I have listed some of them, where appropriate, in a note at the beginning of each chapter, with the warning that length is not in itself a guarantee of high quality). But it seems that there has not hitherto been any concerted attempt to produce an overall assessment of these various aspects of the originality of *Madame Bovary*, and my hope is that this gathering together will make it easier to understand in what ways the work so unmistakably marks a date in the history of the novel. Because it constitutes vital prolegomena to any analysis of *Madame Bovary*, I have thought it necessary to include a study of what preceded it in Flaubert's writing, of the circumstances in which it came to be written, and of his own view of where it stood in relation to existing literature. It also appeared right to give a brief account of the trial and the reception of the novel, since that throws light on the extent to which Flaubert's contemporaries were disconcerted by it and found difficulty in knowing what to make of it.

Quotations from *Madame Bovary* are taken from Claudine Gothot-Mersch's excellent edition (Paris, Garnier, 1971), with page references given in the text. Flaubert's letters are quoted from Jean Bruneau's monumental Pléiade edition (1973–1997). The four volumes to have appeared so far go up to the year 1875, and references are given in the text in the abbreviated form Corr.I, II, III and IV with the page number. Later letters are quoted from the less reliable Club de l'Honnête Homme edition of the *Œuvres complètes*, in the form CHH XV or XVI with the page number. I have adduced quotations from letters written after the completion of *Madame Bovary* because, in my opinion, Flaubert's views on artistic matters changed little if at all once he had started work on that first novel, so that it is legitimate to use later quotations to elucidate this or that aspect of it. Other works by Flaubert are quoted from the Club de l'Honnête Homme edition with the same system of references.

Because *Madame Bovary*, Flaubert's first published work, did not appear until the author was in his mid-thirties, it might be tempting to assume that all the writing he had done in the preceding twenty or more years was by way of preparation for this novel. But while all he had garnered during this period in the way of understanding and presentation of character, in the concatenation of motive and action, in the confection of imagery and in the handling of the French language stood him in good stead when he came to compose *Madame Bovary*, there was little to suggest that his first published novel would be a domestic tragedy set in modern Normandy. Certainly, commentators have found adumbrations of that later work in attitudes to life, in descriptive techniques and even his view of the writing subject. But in terms of the overall conception, one might at most instance *Passion et Vertu* (1837), a dramatic tale of adultery, the satirical *Petite Comédie bourgeoise* intercalated in the 'mystère' *Smarh* (1939), and parts of the novels *Novembre* (1842) and *L'Education sentimentale* (1845). Otherwise the route which leads to *Madame Bovary* is singularly tortuous and unpredictable, and there are many things one will not understand about the novel unless one begins by examining what led up to his starting work on it.

Probably the first fact that one needs to bear in mind is that, however precocious and imperious Flaubert's literary vocation was, it was not in its origins primarily a vocation for narrative fiction, but rather a vocation for the theatre.[8] We have his own word for that in a series of intimate reflections penned in the early or mid 1840s: here is what he wrote:

> Oh mon Dieu, mon Dieu, pourquoi m'avez-vous fait naître avec tant d'ambition – car c'est bien de l'ambition que j'ai – Quand j'avais dix ans, je rêvais déjà la gloire – et j'ai composé dès que j'ai su écrire, je me suis peint tout exprès pour moi de ravissants tableaux – je songeais à une salle pleine de lumières et d'or à des mains qui battent à des cris à

des couronnes – On appelle l'auteur – l'auteur – c'est moi, c'est mon nom moi – moi – on me cherche dans les couloirs, dans les loges, on se penche pour me voir – la toile se lève et je m'avance – quel enivrement! on te regarde, on t'envie on est près de t'aimer de t'avoir vu.[9]

It is well known that for a period of five or more years before and after 1830 Flaubert was the leading light in a group of children who organised amateur theatricals in the billiard-room of the Hôtel-Dieu in Rouen where his father was chief surgeon. Some of the plays they put on were classics – Molière, Carmontelle and others – but many were composed by the young Gustave. Not content with being director, manager, playwright for these productions, he also delighted in playing parts. Indeed, he developed a propensity, which was to remain with him for the rest of his life, for acting out imaginary roles, on or off stage, giving readings for his friends and family from Molière, Hugo or his own writings, or pretending to be fantastic characters he had invented for himself.

As for the plays he composed, most if not all of them at first seem to have been comedies, though in the early 1830s his ambition turned more to the Romantic costume drama in the manner of Hugo or Musset, and he somehow gained access to a twice-weekly theatrical publication entitled *Art et Progrès revue de théâtre*, from which he regularly culled titbits of gossip about Parisian productions which he passed on to his friend Ernest Chevalier. He soon persuaded Chevalier to found with him their own theatrical news-sheet with the imitative title *Art et Progrès. Les soirées d'études. Journal littéraire*. But as only one number has survived, it is not known how long this enterprise lasted.[10]

It is true that, at the same time as Flaubert was planning or writing all these plays, he was also experimenting extensively with narrative fiction, and we know of a large number of stories which he wrote in the 1830s. Nevertheless, it is clear that up to 1838, when he was sixteen, he spent more time on writing for the theatre than on straightforward narratives. Not only that, but several at least of his dramatic projects were for full-scale five-act dramas: in 1835 an apparently unrealised scenario for a five-act imbroglio of passion, murder and adultery, under the title *Deux Amours et un cercueil*,[11] the same year a sanguinary medieval drama *Frédégonde et Brunehaut*, which seems to have been completed and which he even thought of publishing,[12] and in 1838, *Loys XI*, a historical drama in five acts with a prologue, set in the fifteenth century. It is noteworthy that he was prepared to envisage dramas on an epic scale, whereas the pieces of narration never seem to have been destined to occupy more than a few pages. While he does occasionally in this period use the term 'romans' to describe these efforts, in his boyish vocabulary the word does not appear to refer anything more elaborate than a story rather than a play.[13]

It was only in the late 1830s that two works he happened to read affected him so deeply as to change the direction of his intentions. The first of these was Goethe's *Faust*, which he first came across at Easter 1838, and which so enthralled him that, reading it as he came out of school, he became so immersed in it that, instead of returning to his parents' house, he found himself miles away, under pouring rain.[14] The other work, of a similar nature, was Edgar Quinet's version of the myth of the Wandering Jew, *Ahasvérus. Faust* and *Ahasvérus* have in common that they use a pseudo-dramatic form to explore the mysteries of the human condition, without any thought of scenic practicalities. That these works should have held a particular appeal for the adolescent Flaubert is understandable if one bears in mind the peculiarities of *Loys XI*, the first three acts of which are a conventional historical drama, covering decades of violent action. But at this time Flaubert was increasingly preoccupied with metaphysical questions about death and nothingness, and the last two acts of the play contain little by way of dramatic movement, being almost entirely concerned with the ailing king's terror of death. Clearly, such themes do not lend themselves to theatrical exploitation, and Flaubert was evidently delighted to discover, in *Faust* and *Ahasvérus*, a quasi-dramatic form which would enable him to pursue his philosophical meditations without the necessity of weaving them into a plausible dramatic plot.

The result of this discovery is two works of similar character, *La Danse des morts* (1838) and *Smarh* (begun in late 1838 and completed in the spring of 1839). Both compositions have symbolic figures at their centre and both employ a nominally dramatic structure. But both differ from the works by Goethe and Quinet which inspired them in that they incorporate passages of narration and description couched in the past tense. This inconsistent mixture of past and present in these hybrid works brings them a little closer to the genre of narrative fiction than either *Faust* or *Ahasvérus*; they nevertheless remain more closely related to a type of metaphysical 'drame total',[15] with confrontations between Satan, Yuk the spirit of the grotesque, and a wide variety of representative figures: the tone of both is cynical and despairing, and though *Smarh* is developed more consequentially, both works suffer from a disconnected and sporadic structure, in which scenes follow one another without any very clear logical connection. Obviously, *La Danse des Morts* is essentially an experiment, a dress-rehearsal, but one which struck its author as sufficiently effective to be worth repeating and developing on a larger scale in *Smarh* (which in turn can be seen as a kind of forerunner of *La Tentation de Saint Antoine*). In the event, however, after *Smarh* Flaubert for some time abandoned dramatic and quasi-dramatic form, and turned his attention instead to narrative fiction.

The reasons for this change of direction may well have been personal rather than literary or ideological. Already in 1838, Flaubert had written the *Mémoires d'un Fou*, an overt if heavily fictionalised account of his love for Elisa Schlesinger, whom he had met at Trouville in 1836 and for whom he had supposedly conceived a great if undeclared passion.[16] Then in 1841 and 1842 he had written another strongly autobiographical work, *Novembre*, this time based on his sexual encounter with Eulalie Foucaud de Langlade, who had become his mistress in Marseille in 1840. One has the impression that, as he grew towards adulthood, he felt the need to explore and exploit in fictional form his most significant emotional experiences, the more so as he had obviously read a great deal of the confessional literature rife in the Romantic period. Then, in February 1843, he started work on another even more ambitious novel, the first *Education sentimentale*, which, after various interruptions, he completed in January 1845. This first *Education* is

14

the most substantial composition he had yet attempted, but whereas *Novembre* is compact and well planned, *L'Education* is sprawling, uncertain in its direction and excessively disparate in its invention, possibly because his intentions changed, maybe more than once, during its gestation. The opening sentence of the novel identifies Henry as 'le héros de ce livre' (CHH, t.8, p.31), and it is possible that Flaubert's original idea was the Balzacian notion of a determined young provincial making his way in the world of Paris. But either before he started writing, or in the course of composition, he decided he needed a second hero as contrast and so conceived the idea of the more artistically minded budding playwright Jules: 'Un des deux personnages isolé serait faible. Je n'avais d'abord eu l'idée que de celui d'Henry. La nécessité d'un repoussoir m'a fait concevoir celui de Jules' (Corr., II, p.29). But whether or not the character of Jules was in Flaubert's mind before he set pen to paper, it is clear that, as work on the novel progressed, his interest in Henry waned as that in Jules increased. The result is that by the end of the novel Henry is a rather ordinary if socially successful young man, while Jules has become a 'grave et grand artiste' (CHH, t.8, p.244), whose aesthetic ideas are those of Flaubert and whose artistic preferences and views on truth and beauty, form and content were to be staple elements of his creator's thought for the rest of his life. But while Flaubert is extremely serious in his account of Jules's artistic vocation, he is curiously vague about its exact nature. Jules apparently dreams more about success in the theatre than he devotes himself to writing plays. This vagueness is perhaps designed to elude the notorious difficulty of giving in a novel a convincing account of some imaginary masterpiece. It may be too that at this stage Flaubert was uncertain about where his own literary vocation was going to take him.

But it is not only the indecisiveness of the conclusion that betrays a certain infirmity of purpose on Flaubert's part regarding the future direction of his literary career. Though the closing chapters lay the foundations for his mature aesthetic, the novel itself is strangely disparate, as though the author had not fully made up his mind what sort of work he wished to produce, so that its diverse parts and tones fail to coalesce into a coherent whole. Flaubert himself was not unaware of this disconnectedness, and later confessed to Louise Colet:

> En résumé, il faudrait pour *L'Education* récrire ou du moins recaler l'ensemble, refaire deux ou trois chapitres et, ce qui me paraît le plus difficile de tout, écrire un chapitre qui manque, où l'on montrerait comment fatalement le même tronc a dû se bifurquer, c'est-à-dire pourquoi telle action a amené ce résultat dans ce personnage plutôt que telle autre. Les causes sont montrées, les résultats aussi; mais l'enchaînement de la cause à l'effet ne l'est point. Voilà le vice du livre, et comment il ment à son titre (Corr., t.II, p.30).

The lack of consistency is just as marked, if not more so, in the contrast between incompatible styles. The caricatural frivolity of some of the earlier scenes jars with the evident earnestness of Jules's aesthetic meditations towards the end. The convincing depiction of life in the provincial town which Henry and Jules inhabit shows up the poverty of the description of New York when Henry goes there with Mme Renaud (it is painfully obvious that when Flaubert could not rely on personal experience for description, his imagination was – at this stage – incapable of filling in the gap). Moreover, we have not only the straightforward narration which occupies most of the novel and the thoughtful analysis of aesthetic principles towards the end, there is also almost a whole chapter in dialogue form, set out like a scene in a play, satirising the bourgeois stupidities of Henry's parents. Overall, one has the impression that the author has sought to combine in a single work several of the different novel genres popular in the first half of the nineteenth century: the sentimental love story in the parallel threads of Jules's unhappy passion for the actress Lucinde and Henry's affair with Mme Renaud, the comic and satirical novel in the scenes in the Renaud boarding-house, the novel of artistic vocation in the account of Jules's aesthetic speculations. So, although some commentators are disposed to see the 1845 *Education* as Flaubert's first great novel and though Jean Bruneau has good grounds for writing: 'Flaubert a jeté les bases sur lesquelles il fondera son œuvre [...] il ne lui reste plus qu'à se

16

mettre à l'œuvre. [...] mais le monde ne connaîtra cette révolution littéraire que dix ans plus tard, quand paraîtra *Madame Bovary*,[17] the fact is that the first *Education sentimentale* is a seriously flawed work, and that there is a long and complex way to go before Flaubert is in a position to compose *Madame Bovary*.

In the meantime, while he was working on *L'Education*, Flaubert's personal circumstances had changed fatefully, when early in 1844 he had the first of the seizures which were to plague him for a number of years. The immediate result of this medically mysterious illness was the abandonment of the legal studies which, at his father's behest, he was reluctantly pursuing in Paris, and the return to the parental home in Croisset to convalesce. Though the seizures gradually grew less frequent, it soon became apparent that there could be no question of Flaubert following a normal career in the law or any other profession which would keep him in the public eye. So it seems to have been agreed, tacitly or formally, that he could remain at home and devote himself to his passion for writing. Thus by the summer of 1845 he was in a mood of unexpected serenity: 'Ma maladie aura toujours eu l'avantage qu'on me laisse m'occuper comme je l'entends, ce qui est un grand point dans la vie' (Corr., t.I, p.214); 'Je vis d'une façon réglée, calme, régulière, m'occupant exclusivement de littérature et d'histoire' (Corr., t.I, p.249). But if Achille-Cléophas, Gustave's surgeon father, seems to have accepted that, under the circumstances, the best thing for his son was to become a man of letters, he no doubt had his own opinion as to what precisely that implied. Though he was a cultivated man, far from the philistine depicted by Maxime Du Camp,[18] his tastes in literature were essentially conservative, and so, after the débâcle of *Les Burgraves* in 1843, when the Romantic theatre appeared to be on the way out, it is probable that he encouraged Gustave to apply himself to preparing for a revival of the neo-Classical theatre. This seems to be the only plausible explanation for the task on which Gustave embarked in the summer of 1845 and which he continued assiduously for several months. This was the elaborate summarising and commenting on Voltaire's theatre (72 volumes of Voltaire's works formed part of the father's library). Flaubert had an enormous admiration for

Voltaire's tales, but he patently detested his plays, and his comments are almost invariably extremely hostile, save when he detects in the dramas or prefaces some vague adumbration of Romantic theatre. 33 plays are thus dissected in 458 pages of notes (which are not even spontaneous, but redrafts of the notes he took as he read). He has nothing but scorn for the artificiality of the plays, the stilted language, the clumsy lines, the implausible characters and the constant expression of Voltaire's own opinions. Though he hypocritically claimed to his friend Alfred Le Poittevin that he believed this work would be useful to him later on (Corr., t.I, p.247), it is obvious that he knew it could not be, save in the purely negative sense of showing him some traps to avoid, especially since only weeks before devoting himself to this absurd and thankless task, he had produced a brief sketch for a historical drama on the Corsican condottiere San Pietro Ornano, which would certainly have borne more resemblance to *Loys XI* than to any of Voltaire's tragedies.[19] One can only assume that this time-consuming and useless activity of annotating Voltaire's theatre was a way of convincing his father, of whom as a powerful and domineering figure he was in awe, that his intentions as a budding dramatist were respectable and required a long and arduous training. But his true opinion of Voltaire's theatre is summed up a few years later in a single word: 'Pitoyable' (Corr., t.II, p.417).[20]

Unsurprisingly, after the death of Achille-Cléophas in January 1846, there is no further mention of the theatre of Voltaire: with the old surgeon no longer alive, there was no reason for Flaubert to keep up the futile pretence that he was going to revive the neo-Classical drama. But while the disappearance of Achille-Cléophas was no doubt for Flaubert something of a liberation, despite all the affection he felt for him, very shortly afterwards, a second traumatic event reduced Flaubert to a state of disarray in which there could be no more question of literary enterprises; this was the death, after childbirth, of his much loved younger sister Caroline. The after-effects of this second bereavement were almost at once complicated when Emile Hamard, Caroline's widower, began showing signs of mental derangement and started a lawsuit against the Flaubert family to win the guardianship of Caroline, the

18

daughter born to Flaubert's sister just before her death. At the same time, Gustave became actively involved in the intrigues designed to secure the appointment of his elder brother Achille in succession to his father as chief surgeon of the Hôtel-Dieu in Rouen. It is hardly surprising that amid all these upheavals literature should for the time being have been pushed to the back of Gustave's preoccupations.

So it was not for some time that any new literary project surfaced, and even then it seems to have been an idea intended as much to enable him to set pen to paper again as a major artistic enterprise. This was the plan of a tour of Brittany with his friend Maxime Du Camp, which lasted from May to August 1847 and to which his mother reluctantly consented, on the grounds that it might be good for his health now that his attacks were recurring less often. But in addition to getting to know a province so remote and isolated that it virtually ranked as a foreign country, the two young writers had another intention, which was to give themselves a thorough training in the discipline of observation and description, important at that time not only for the novel but even more for the very popular genre of travel-writing. The idea was that the two men should write alternate chapters, if possible during the journey, or, if not, after their return on the basis of the notes they had taken. There does not appear to have been any serious question of publication, which personal remarks and private jokes would have rendered impossible. In the event, though Flaubert for the first time wrote slowly and painfully, he finished his chapters before Du Camp, who patently attached less seriousness to the whole enterprise. The training in the exact rendering of what Flaubert had seen and experienced undoubtedly proved invaluable, and without it description would certainly not have played the vital part it did in his subsequent novels.[21] This training in the art of observation and description was later deepened and extended by the elaborate notes he took on what he saw on his travels in the Middle East, Greece and Italy in 1849–1851, posthumously published under the title *Voyage en Orient*.

Once he had completed this exercise, for that is above all what it was, Flaubert began to turn his attention to the preparation of a major work of imagination, and two possibilities lodged in his mind, both of them originally conceived early in 1845 but left in abeyance because of the intervening events. One was inspired by a Breughel painting which had fascinated him when he saw it in Italy.[22] 'J'ai vu un tableau de Breughel représentant *La Tentation de Saint Antoine*, qui m'a fait penser à arranger pour le théâtre *La Tentation de Saint Antoine*. Mais cela demanderait un autre gaillard que moi' (Corr., t.I, p.230), as he told Alfred Le Poittevin in May 1845. The other was an oriental novel to be entitled *Les Sept Fils du derviche*, which would have recounted the lives of seven brothers in the Middle East in ancient times.[23] Flaubert appears to have started on the Eastern tale before, in late 1846, launching into a vast programme of reading for *La Tentation*. Both works would have incorporated into a structure of epic dimensions a whole vision of the world and a philosophy of life, drawing on prolonged study of religions and exotic subjects. According to Jean Bruneau's plausible hypothesis,[24] Flaubert was at first so discouraged by the problems he foresaw in any sort of dramatic presentation of *La Tentation* that he favoured the oriental tale, until he realised that, having had no direct contact with the inhabitants, the customs and the scenery of the Middle East, he was ill-equipped to evoke it convincingly. In addition, having decided to set the story in times of which there was no historical record, he would be unable to deal in it with Christianity and its attendant heresies to which his reading had turned his interest. Consequently, although he continued to note ideas for the novel and worked on it more consistently after his return from the Middle East in 1851, he decided to give priority to *La Tentation*.

Preliminary reading for it had begun late in 1846, but work was interrupted by the travels in Brittany and subsequent composition of *Par les champs et par les grèves*, the death of his close friend Alfred Le Poittevin in April 1848 and the vicissitudes of his stormy relationship with Louise Colet. So it was only on May 24 1848 that he finally sat down and started writing. For the next sixteen months he went on composing with great fluency and enthusiasm until at last on September 12 1849, he reached the end. The importance he attached to the work, which he clearly regarded as his first really serious literary enterprise is shown by the fact that, contrary to his usual practice, he absolutely refused to tell his closest friends Maxime Du Camp and Louis Bouilhet anything about it, so that when, in the autumn of 1849, he invited them to Croisset for a solemn reading of the completed work, they had little or no idea of what to expect, though they realised that Flaubert attached enormous importance to what he had achieved.

There is little direct evidence about what happened at the reading, apart from Du Camp's account, many years later, in his *Souvenirs littéraires*. It is beyond doubt that some of the details he gives are mistaken; it is beyond doubt too that, in everything Du Camp wrote about Flaubert, one can detect a sour if repressed jealousy which leads him to angle his reminiscences so as to present the other as obsessional, unreasonable and arrested in his development by his nervous illness. But, allowing for that, there are good grounds, both general and particular, for believing that Du Camp remained as faithful to the facts as he could be.

According to what Du Camp relates, the reading lasted four days, with two four-hour sessions each day, and with an agreement that the two listeners would not reveal their reactions until the end. Flaubert must no doubt have sensed in advance that their opinion was not the acclamation on which he had counted: he must nevertheless have been devastated when Bouilhet said: 'Nous pensons qu'il faut jeter cela au feu et n'en jamais reparler'.[25] The reasons for this categorical condemnation were multiple: it was far too long, the style might be magnificent but was prolix and disordered, the logic for the sequence of episodes was incomprehensible, Antoine was not an interesting character. However much Flaubert may at first have have been inclined to dismiss these criticisms, it is clear that over a period of months if not years, he came to recognise that they were not unjustified: as he admitted on various occasions, he had paid insufficient attention to the thread linking the different episodes (Corr., t.II,p.31); the planning had been inadequate (Corr., t.II, p.41); and he had identified too completely with Antoine (Corr., t.II, p.30). What Bouilhet and Du Camp suggested to counteract these damaging tendencies was to take a subject down-to-earth and closely connected to daily life, so that excessive lyricism would be unthinkable. Again, if we are to believe Du Camp, the two friends advised him: 'Prends un sujet terre à terre, quelque chose comme *Le Cousin Pons* ou *La Cousine Bette* de Balzac',[26] and suggested to him that he might use as his model the story of the Delamare family from the little Norman village of Ry, where the wife Delphine, after taking lovers, had committed suicide. But here Du Camp is certainly wrong, since in 1849 the widower Delamare was still alive and it would have been patently impossible to use this domestic tragedy as the basis for a novel. That at some later date Flaubert did decide to use the Delamare story as the distant base of his novel is proven, because in July 1851 Du Camp wrote asking him: 'Est-ce toujours Don Juan? [a subject Flaubert had been contemplating since at least the previous April] est-ce l'histoire de Mme Delamare qui est bien belle?' (Corr., t.II, p.859) By the beginning of August his decision was taken, and the title *Madame Bovary* invented. The first scenarios were produced in August and September, and on September 19 he began the actual writing which went on, without major interruptions but with painful slowness, until March 1856. After that, and after signing a contract for the serialisation of the novel in Du Camp's *Revue de Paris*, he had to have his manuscript copied out by a professional copyist so that it could be dispatched to Du Camp on May 31 1856. The serialisation, in monthly instalments, lasted from October to December 1856.

Mindful of the reproaches which Bouilhet and Du Camp had addressed to *La Tentation*, Flaubert adopted a radically new technique for the composition of *Madame Bovary*. After establishing a series of general plans for the novel as a whole, he then produced more detailed plans for each section of it (not for each chapter, since the division into chapters is only effected on the copyist's manuscript) before writing it up. There was also a constant labour of revision, which continued even onto the copyist's manuscript and beyond, since there were further corrections to the proofs of the *Revue de Paris*. Late in December, he sold the rights for publication in book form to Michel Lévy, so that the book appeared, in two volumes, in April 1857. It had thus taken between five and six years for the work to reach its final form, and it seems certain that never before had a novel been so meticulously planned and its style so minutely elaborated. Probably hitherto only an epic poem had so much time and care lavished on it.

II   Flaubert's view of *Madame Bovary*

It is thus clear that *Madame Bovary* was a project on which Flaubert embarked unwillingly, that it was totally unlike anything he had attempted before, and indeed that it was largely conceived as a corrective to the defects and excesses he had been led to recognise in *La Tentation*, a work which he regarded as much more representative of his true talent. It is nevertheless instructive to see how in 1851 and the following years Flaubert situated himself in relation to the evolution of literature in general and the novel in particular. His great literary admirations were established at an early age and varied little, if at all, thereafter: Homer, Apuleius, Shakespeare, Cervantes, Rabelais, Montaigne, Chateaubriand and Hugo. But it is noteworthy that, even at the outset, he appears never to have seen himself as following in the footsteps of any of these masters. It was common in the nineteenth century for young writers to seek to emulate or displace one or other of the great authors of a previous generation: one thinks of Hugo's proud ambition: 'Je veux être Chateaubriand ou rien',[27] of Balzac hoping to have 'arraché la palme du roman à Walter Scott',[28] or Villiers de l'Isle-Adam proposing to ascend to the 'trône de la pensée' occupied by Hugo.[29] In all the voluminous correspondence of Flaubert's youth, one never finds him seeking to define himself by reference to any writer of the past or present.

This is of course not to say that the juvenilia are anything other than derivative, and in the early plays and stories there are many reminiscences of Mérimée, Hoffmann, Pétrus Borel, his friend Le Poittevin and others. But as he approached maturity, he gives the impression of seeking to distance himself from any predecessors, and in this respect the case of *Novembre* is particularly revealing. It is apparent that in writing this work he had in mind two great novels for which he had an especial affection: Goethe's *Werther* and Chateaubriand's *René*. It is almost certainly *Werther* which gives him the idea of a first-person narration breaking off so that a third party can give an account from the outside of the hero's decline and death. As for *René*, there is at least one obvious imitation of a celebrated lyrical outburst,[30] and *Novembre* has in common with both novels an exploration of metaphysical despair and amorous passion. There are also echoes of the tormented sensuality of Amaury, the hero of Sainte-Beuve's *Volupté*, which Flaubert had read while still at school.[31] But despite these precedents, Flaubert was jealously protective of his independence in *Novembre*. When he read the novel to Maxime Du Camp, the author asked his friend: 'A quoi trouves-tu que cela ressemble?', Du Camp replied hesitantly but flatteringly: 'Ça rappelle un peu la manière de Théophile Gautier', only to be put in his place by the sharp reply: 'Tu te trompes, ça ne ressemble à rien'.[32] Several years later, Louise Colet fared no better when she made so bold as to compare *Novembre* to *René* and was notably disconcerted to receive this acerbic response:

> Oui, je repense souvent à la soirée de *Novembre*, et aux pleurs que tu versais quand tu faisais des allusions involontaires; mais je n'en persiste pas moins à croire que tu estimes cela trop. J'ai été même indigné que tu aies comparé ce livre à *René*. Ça m'a semblé une profanation. Pouvais-je te le dire, puisque c'était une preuve d'amour? (Corr., t.I, p.417).

So taken aback was Louise by this reaction that Du Camp was moved to try to console her: '[Flaubert] a été profondément blessé des éloges que vous avez faits de *Novembre*: non pas qu'il ait cru que vous vouliez vous moquer, mais parce qu'il admire profondément *René*, et qu'à juste titre il se trouvait fort inférieur au plus grand chef-d'œuvre de l'esprit humain' (Corr., t.I, p.1022). It is of course true that Flaubert harboured a deep veneration of Chateaubriand, and it is also true that the comparison of *Novembre* to Théophile Gautier is not particularly apt. To that extent, his refusal of the parallels proposed by Du Camp and Louise Colet may have been sincere. At the same time, one cannot help feeling that he resented being compared to anyone and wanted to believe that what he wrote was unique.

The case of the 1845 *Education sentimentale* is different. We have already pointed out the diversity of his intentions in this novel and the disparities which that entails. The dialogue of Chapter XXIII unmistakably imitates the satirical scenes which were a speciality of Henry Monnier, whom Flaubert had read (or seen on the stage) and admired. As a novel of artistic apprenticeship, it perhaps owes something to Goethe's *Wilhelm Meister*, though only in its latter stages, since Flaubert does not seem to have known the work before Du Camp recommended it to him in May 1844.[33] It is possible too, since the novel opens with Henry leaving his provincial home town and arriving to make his way in Paris that Flaubert had some thought of a novel along Balzacian lines, with Henry as a latter-day Eugène de Rastignac or Lucien de Rubempré, but, if so, that intention must have got lost as the novel evolved. Indeed, Maurice Bardèche is positively indignant that Flaubert should have failed to follow Balzac's example at this point in his career:

> cette *Education sentimentale* est son premier pas dans une direction toute différente, celle du roman [...]. Un roman, et quel roman! non pas Balzac, non pas Walter Scott, auxquels un débutant de vingt-deux ans pouvait aspirer à ressembler, même pas le sérieux des caudataires de Balzac, un Félix Davin ou un Samuel-Henry Berthoud: mais Paul de Kock, Auguste Ricard ou Pigault-Lebrun.[34]

It is true that Maxime Du Camp reveals that Flaubert had a somewhat shamefaced liking for the unpretentious comic novels of Pigault-Lebrun, 'qu'il avait lu, qui le faisait rire et l'avait poussé vers une recherche du comique dont le résultat n'a pas toujours été heureux'.[35] Certainly the frivolously humorous scenes which abound in the recital of Henry's misadventures in the Renaud boarding-house recall the manner of Pigault-Lebrun, but the multiplicity of Flaubert's intentions in *L'Education* means that it is hardly possible to attribute to him the aim of emulating any single writer.

The influence of Quinet and Goethe, already apparent in *La Danse des Morts* and *Smarh*, continues to dominate in the 1849 *Tentation*, though the extent and recondite nature of Flaubert's vast preparatory reading make that work very different from either *Faust* or *Ahasvérus*. But the condemnation of the *Tentation* by Du Camp and Bouilhet meant that Flaubert was obliged to rethink in its entirety his approach to literature, so that little survived of what had gone before apart from the aesthetic principles evolved in *L'Education*.

Those principles were not dependent on allegiance to any particular modern novelists. Most of the writers Flaubert revered offered little in the way of guidance for a nineteenth-century novelist, the more so as he regarded the novel as essentially a new genre which was still in process of finding its way. As he was to write in 1852: 'je crois que le roman ne fait que de naître, il attend son Homère' (Corr., t.II, p.209). Consequently, although there were novelists whom he ranked highly – in the eighteenth century, Sterne, Bernardin de Saint-Pierre, Prévost, Lesage, and more recently Chateaubriand and Goethe – they did not offer much in the way of practical inspiration. But despite his admiration for Chateaubriand's style (which he imitated adroitly and successfully when he wanted to create an atmosphere of emotional elevation), Chateaubriand's Catholicism prevented him from seeing him as a possible model. Something similar is true of Scott, – whose moralising and occasionally cavalier attitude to history shocked him; in any case, by the 1840s Scott's picturesque medievalism had become a hackneyed cliché (as is evinced by the part his novels play in forming Emma's naïve dream world). As for Stendhal, Flaubert was totally out of sympathy with him and averred that for the life of him he could not understand why Balzac admired such a man.[36]

This meant that, among modern novelists, the only one who might have offered something of a model was Balzac, and we have seen that it was under the aegis of Balzac that Du Camp and Bouilhet urged Flaubert to turn away from the manner of *La Tentation*. But the attitude of Flaubert toward Balzac was extremely complex, compounded of awe before his immense achievement in depicting the society of his time and irritation with his mishandling of the French language and constant expounding of his own opinions, most of which, like his royalism and his Catholicism, were anathema to Flaubert.[37] So, while Flaubert reluctantly accepted the necessity for taking an everyday subject from contemporary life like those of *La Comédie humaine*, there was no way in which he was going to try to produce the same sort of novel as Balzac had. Admittedly, there are analogies between the themes and settings of *Madame Bovary* and those of certain Balzac novels: *La Muse du département*,[38] *Le Médecin de campagne*,[39] *Eugénie Grandet*[40] and *La Rabouilleuse*[41] have all been adduced in this connection, but in no case does the parallel bear on more than detail or a vague similarity of situation. Flaubert himself was anxious to emphasise the differences: while accepting that a scene in *Madame Bovary* presented analogies with one in *Le Médecin de campagne* (which he declared he had not read), he at once insisted that the quality of style made all the difference: 'Ce sont *mêmes détails*, mêmes effets, même intention, à croire que j'ai copié, si ma page n'était infiniment mieux écrite, sans me vanter' (Corr., t.II, p.219). Indeed, the text of *Madame Bovary* itself contains an oblique criticism of Balzac, which was very much more explicit in the drafts. This occurs when Flaubert is detailing the unrealistic picture of life in Paris which Emma has culled from her unsophisticated reading of George Sand, Eugène Sue and Balzac. Contrary to what one might expect, her errors derive principally from Balzac rather than from the other two, and after having produced a list of the strata of Parisian society as imagined by Emma after the *Scènes de la vie parisienne*, Flaubert concludes abruptly: 'Pas question des bourgeois'.[42] Obviously, Flaubert was perfectly well aware of the dominance of bourgeois figures in the *Comédie humaine*, and even the imperceptive Emma can hardly have failed to notice their presence. What he had in mind is that Balzac refuses to depict bourgeois characters in their mediocrity and platitude: he magnifies and transforms them, so that, for example, the petty perfumer César Birotteau becomes the paragon of 'probité commerciale',[43] thereby escaping the anonymity of his fellows and appearing as a unique and exceptional individual. A phrase of the drafts makes explicit what Flaubert reproaches Balzac with: 'poétisation du vulgaire – célébrité pareille répandue sur tout'.[44] Years later, the same objection was formulated in *Bouvard et Pécuchet*: 'ses bourgeois ne sont pas des bourgeois, mais des colosses. Pourquoi gonfler ce qui est plat, et décrire tant de sottises?' (CHH, t.V, p.138). (Admittedly, this opinion is attributed to Flaubert's 'deux bonshommes', but, especially in the section on literature, one finds among their misapprehensions and stupidity many remarks which directly reflect their creator's own views).

It is thus abundantly clear that, while Flaubert recognised that his novel would in some respects be attached to a Balzacian tradition, he had absolutely no intention of writing a Balzacian-type work. As early as September 1851, he summed up his dilemma in these words: 'Ce n'est pas une petite affaire que d'être simple. J'ai peur de tomber dans le Paul de Kock ou de faire du Balzac chateaubrianisé' (Corr., t.II, p.5). In other words, the main dangers were using an inappropriately elevated style to evoke ordinary realities (which would be rewriting Balzac in the manner of Chateaubriand), or, on the other hand, failing to make the necessary stylistic effort and ending up with a product which would have no more literary distinction than the popular chronicles of middle-class life by Paul de Kock.

In the event, and whatever Flaubert's desire to distinguish what he was doing from what Balzac had done, when *Madame Bovary* appeared critics and readers were almost unanimous in relating it to the Balzacian model – and this whether they admired or detested the novel. Those who disapproved of it accused it of the immorality with which Balzac had often been taxed; thus Flaubert's father's colleague Dr. Hellis wrote to a friend: 'Il [Flaubert] vient d'en publier un [roman] [...] Il singe Balzac: qu'il l'imite dans sa finesse, son coup de pinceaux et son style, mais qu'il ne glorifie pas le vice et la turpitude'.[45] The others saw in Flaubert the worthy successor of Balzac: his friend Louis de Cormenin declared: '*Madame Bovary* restera, car après l'avoir lue, on s'apercevra que Balzac a laissé un héritier. Gustave Flaubert!'.[46] Congratulating Flaubert, the novelist and critic Edmond About averred that the novel was like Balzac, but better written, more passionate and cleaner,[47] while Balzac's friend Léon Gozlan claimed that he had thought of Balzac all the time he was reading it. George Sand, who did not know Flaubert at the time, concluded that it was like Balzac, only freed of all concession to melodrama, more bitter and more concentrated.[48] Given Flaubert's unwillingness to be seen as the new Balzac, it is not surprising that, far from being flattered by these comparisons, he was furious with them: 'Quant au Balzac, j'en ai décidément les oreilles cornées. Je vais tâcher de leur triple-ficeler quelque chose de rutilant et de gueulard où le rapprochement ne sera plus facile. Sont-ils bêtes avec leurs observations de mœurs! Je me fous bien de ça!' (Corr., t.II, p.727).

It may of course be argued that Flaubert himself fostered this misunderstanding by allowing the novel to be published with the subtitle *Mœurs de province*, clearly intended to recall Balzac's *Etudes de mœurs* and *Scènes de la vie de province*. But the history of this subtitle is curious. It does not figure on Flaubert's own manuscript and only appears on the copyist's manuscript, where it is inserted, not in Flaubert's hand, but apparently in that of Maxime Du Camp, in his capacity as co-editor of the *Revue de Paris*, where it was serialised. It is true that Flaubert raised no objection to this, and that when a pre-publication advertisement was printed in that form, his only reaction was to ironise about the mis-spelling of his own name; it is also true that the subtitle is maintained in all the editions which came out in his lifetime, when, if he had wanted to get rid of it, there was nothing to stop him doing so (possibly he allowed it to ride because he thought it could be read ironically). However that may be, one cannot contend that Flaubert repudiated the idea of *Madame Bovary* as a study of 'mœurs de province', but one can demonstrate that this conception of the work was not uppermost in his mind while he was writing it, and that it was therefore legitimate for him to protest that the purpose of the novel was absolutely not to constitute a series of 'observations de mœurs'.

The fact is that, if one studies the hundreds of known letters that Flaubert wrote while working on *Madame Bovary*, one finds that he never seeks to characterise his novel by reference to existing literature, other than by protesting that it will not be more Balzac or more Paul de Kock, or that it will be better than Champfleury's *Les Bourgeois de Molinchart* or Du Camp's *Livre posthume*. On the contrary, he regularly stresses its uniqueness and its originality. Obviously, we shall be examining in detail later the various aspects of that originality, but it is perhaps relevant and valuable at this stage to quote some of the declarations which demonstrate Flaubert's consciousness of the extent to which what he was attempting was unprecedented and groundbreaking. To Louise Colet in 1852: 'Toute la valeur de mon livre, s'il en a une, sera d'avoir su marcher droit sur un cheveu, suspendu entre le double abîme du lyrisme et du vulgaire (que je veux fondre dans une analyse narrative). Quand je pense à ce que ça peut être, j'en ai des éblouissements' (Corr., t.II, p.57); or to the same correspondent a few months later: 'Il ne me paraît pas non plus impossible de donner à l'analyse psychologique la rapidité, la netteté, l'emportement d'une narration purement dramatique. Cela n'a jamais été tenté et serait beau. Y ai-je réussi un peu? Je n'en sais rien' (Corr., t.II, p.136); or again to Louise, the following year: 'Vouloir donner à la prose le rythme du vers (en la laissant prose et très prose) et écrire la vie ordinaire comme on écrit l'histoire et l'épopée (sans dénaturer le sujet) est peut-être une absurdité. Voilà ce que je me demande parfois. Mais c'est peut-être aussi une grande tentative et très originale!' (Corr., t.II, p.287).

But before going on to examine more precisely in what ways *Madame Bovary* is a new departure in the history of the novel, it is necessary to look at an aspect of the work which aroused enormous controversy at the time of its publication and which for long bedevilled the proper understanding and appreciation of its qualities. That is the question of its morality, which would no doubt have arisen anyway, but which was thrown into prominence by the Imperial Government's decision to prosecute it for offences against morality and religion.

III   The scandal

The impact made by *Madame Bovary* and at least its short-term reputation were immeasurably affected by the circumstances of its publication, and for that reason it is essential to examine the events surrounding its appearance. The *Revue de Paris*, of which Du Camp was one of the co-editors, was primarily a literary periodical, originally founded in 1839 but having ceased to appear in 1844. In 1851 it was revived by a group of writers, including Théophile Gautier, Arsène Houssaye and Louis de Cormenin as well as Du Camp, and in addition to *Madame Bovary* it published *Melaenis*, the first major work by Louis Bouilhet. Though the review was theoretically apolitical, it was viewed with suspicion by the Imperial government, extremely touchy and authoritarian in the years following the Coup d'Etat, and in April 1856 had already received two official warnings about what had appeared in it. Du Camp and Laurent-Pichat, who was a major shareholder, had by then taken over as the managing editors and were consequently very worried that the subject-matter of Flaubert's novel might get them into further trouble, which, under the draconian censorship laws then in force, would automatically have resulted in the suppression of the review. A long wrangle ensued with the editors demanding the omission of certain passages deemed likely to upset the authorities and Flaubert resisting tenaciously, to the point of considering taking the *Revue* to court. In the end, the writer was forced to agree to some cuts but became furious when he saw that others had been made without his authorisation and obliged the *Revue* to insert a curt note in which he disclaimed responsibility for the mutilated text. The serialisation nevertheless ran its course, apparently with considerable success, since on December 12 Flaubert commented with satisfaction: 'La *Bovary* marche au-delà de mes espérances' (Corr., t.II, p.652) and on December 20 was able to sign a contract with Michel Lévy for its publication in book form for the sum of 800 francs.

In the meantime, the problems with the censors which the editors of the *Revue de Paris* had feared finally materialised, and on December 27 Du Camp warned Flaubert that a case was pending against the novelist, the printer and Laurent-Pichat for having published a work subverting morality and attacking the Church. Opinions are divided as to what exactly lay behind the decision to prosecute. Flaubert himself was convinced that it was a purely political tactic, designed to provide the government with an excuse for closing down the *Revue*: 'Je suis un prétexte. On veut démolir la *Revue de Paris*, et on me prend pour cogner dessus' (Corr., t.II, p.656). But according to the memoirs of the lawyer charged with presenting the prosecution case, the affair originated simply with an unfavourable report from an official in the censor's department, and this is certainly not impossible, given how violently the regime was liable to react with anything which might seem critical of religion. There is probably some truth in both versions. The *Revue* was already unpopular with the authorities who were no doubt only too happy to take it to court, and conservative opinion could plausibly regard *Madame Bovary* as immoral and irreligious. Flaubert was predictably indignant and immediately set about defending himself and his fellow-accused. His first thought was to try to persuade the government not to bring the case to court, and to this end he sought to mobilise all those who might have influence with the authorities, among others Ernest Le Roy, prefect of the Seine Inférieure, the princesse de Beauvau, the father of the dramatist Emile Augier, his old schoolfellow the journalist Edmond Pagnerre, the minister of Education, and the chief of police. At the same time, he pointed out that the prominent position of the Flaubert family in Rouen meant that to convict him would have very adverse effects on the political fortunes of government candidates when it came to elections. As he wrote to his brother Achille:

> Les renseignements sur la position influente que notre père et que toi a eue et as à Rouen sont tout ce qu'il y a de meilleur; on avait cru s'attaquer à un pauvre bougre, et quand on a vu d'abord que j'avais de quoi vivre on a commencé à ouvrir les yeux. Il faut qu'on sache au Ministère de l'Intérieur que nous sommes à Rouen, ce qui s'appelle *une*

famille, c'est-à-dire que nous avons des racines profondes dans le pays, et qu'en m'attaquant, pour immoralité surtout, on blessera beaucoup de monde (Corr., t.II, p.659).

Flaubert also set about collecting expressions of support from eminent men of letters, attaching particular importance to Lamartine. In addition to activating all his social, political and literary connections, he took the precaution of thinking of arguments in case he failed to deter the government from proceeding with the case.

Chief among his arguments was that the allegedly indecent scenes of *Madame Bovary* were very anodine compared with what could be found in the most respectable classics of French literature – Mérimée, Sainte-Beuve, Balzac, Hugo, even Montesquieu and Rousseau. These arguments were drawn up in consultation with his lawyer Antoine-Marie-Jules Sénard, an old family friend who had occupied important political and legal positions under the July Monarchy and the Second Republic. Several times it appeared that the charges were going to be dropped, but in the end the case was heard on January 29 1857 and judgement delivered on February 7. The accused were all acquitted, but, no doubt as a sop to the government, the judgement included a stern reprimand: 'l'ouvrage déféré au tribunal mérite un blâme sévère'.[49] Flaubert's own attitude in all this was somewhat ambivalent. On the one hand, he was totally indifferent about the moral effect his book might have; as he explained to a cousin during the serialisation: 'La morale de l'Art consiste dans sa beauté même, et j'estime par-dessus tout le style et ensuite le Vrai' (Corr., t.II, p.652). But at other times, even in private, he seems to have half believed that *Madame Bovary* could be considered a cautionary tale:

Je crois avoir fait un livre moral par son effet, par son ensemble. Quant aux détails, on me reproche une extrême-onction qui est copiée presque littéralement sur le Rituel. Le personnage ridicule de mon roman est un voltairien, philosophe matérialiste (comme le Garçon!). – Je ne pense nullement à l'adultère, ni à l'irréligion, puisque je montre, comme tout bon auteur doit faire, la punition de l'inconduite (Corr., t.II, p.657).

This latter position was of course the one which his lawyer was forced to adopt in court. In his speech for the prosecution, Ernest Pinard began by summarising the action of the novel, saying that it could with justification have been entitled *Histoire des adultères d'une femme de province*. He then went on to pick out what he considered the most lascivious scenes and those most offensive to religious susceptibilities, the seduction by Rodolphe, Emma's pseudo-religious phase, her affair with Léon, her suicide, the last rites, claiming that morality is only represented by 'un être grotesque, M.Homais', and religion by the abbé Bournisien, 'à peu près aussi grotesque que le pharmacien'.[50] The speech for the defence opened with a eulogy of the Flaubert family and a brief account of Gustave's seriousness of purpose in depicting life as it is. Then came the inevitable argument that, far from glorifying adultery, the novel showed its sequel of disillusionment and bitterness. A few words of praise for its literary qualities led to emphasis on the fact that it had won the spontaneous appreciation of no less a person than Lamartine. There followed a detailed examination of the passages incriminated by the prosecution, pointing out how reserved they were compared to analogous scenes in accepted works, and submitting that the morality of the novel lay in its overall effect, not in individual scenes or paragraphs. A good deal of this, on both sides, is shadow-boxing. It is difficult to believe that anyone reading *Madame Bovary* could think they were being encouraged to go out and commit adultery, revel in unbridled sensuality or condemn the teachings of the Church. But equally, while Emma ultimately meets a horrible fate, she is never explicitly condemned for her infidelities. To that extent, the whole trial eludes the real issues involved in the work, and centres on questions which it was never intended to raise. Nevertheless, and despite the acquittal, Flaubert was so worried about the rebuke administered by the court and about the possible consequences of restoring the cuts made by the *Revue de Paris* that he hesitated to allow Lévy to go ahead with the publication in book form. Having received assurances that the government had accepted the verdict and was not going to appeal against it, he consented to its appearance, and it was put on sale in April. The first edition of 6750 copies was very soon sold out, and two new editions appeared in 1857, so that Michel Lévy voluntarily paid Flaubert an extra 500 francs.

Probably *Madame Bovary* would have been commercially successful anyway, after the attention it had received during its serialisation, but the publicity aroused by the trial ensured that it was an immediate best-seller: as Maxime Du Camp wrote: 'Le résultat ne fut pas celui que l'administration avait cherché; grâce à cette persécution, au procès en police correctionnelle, au réquisitoire de l'avocat impérial, *Madame Bovary* eut un succès colossal; du jour au lendemain Gustave Flaubert était devenu célèbre'.[51] Flaubert himself had foreseen this outcome even before the trial, writing disrespectfully: 'Je vais devenir le lion de la semaine, toutes les hautes garces s'arrachent la *Bovary* pour y trouver des obscénités qui n'y sont pas' (Corr., t.II, p.658). As was to be expected, critical opinion was sharply divided. Sainte-Beuve, acknowledged to be the most authoritative critic of the day, wrote a long review, taking the novel extremely seriously and praising its structure and its spirit of observation.[52] There were also laudatory reviews from Baudelaire, Louis de Cormenin and Barbey d'Aurevilly (with some reservations). On the other side, there were naturally some ferocious attacks: J. Habans declared that 'M. Flaubert n'est pas un écrivain. Le style est parfois indécis, incorrect et vulgaire';[53] Edmond Duranty, in his periodical *Le Réalisme*, maintained that 'il n'y a ni émotion, ni sentiment, ni vie dans ce roman, mais une grande force d'arithmétique';[54] for Granier de Cassagnac, *Madame Bovary* was nothing so much as 'un gros tas de fumier'.[55] Clearly, there could be no consensus, when moral, political, literary and religious opinions were so widely divergent, and when the trial had provoked such controversy.

A great deal of what was written at the time about *Madame Bovary* nowadays seems simply irrelevant, whether it was unfavourable or otherwise. What is clear is that it bewildered many of its readers, who simply did not know what to make of it. A large number of them, to Flaubert's annoyance, attached it to the tradition of Balzac, whether to salute it or to condemn it. This general surprise tends to confirm what Flaubert himself undoubtedly believed, namely, that *Madame Bovary* was a radically new departure in novel-writing.

IV   Impersonality[56]

According to Jean Bruneau, 'Au début de 1845, Flaubert est arrivé à sa célèbre doctrine de l'impersonnalité'.[57] There is no doubt some exaggeration in this view: it is true that in the concluding section of *L'Education sentimentale*, when we are initiated into Jules's aesthetic meditations, it appears that the young man is adopting a technique designed to prevent him from yielding too easily to the natural bent of his own personality:

> Il s'adonna à l'étude d'ouvrages offrant des caractères différents du sien, et des façons de style qui n'étaient pas du genre de son style. Ce qu'il aimait à trouver, c'était le développement d'une personnalité féconde, l'expansion d'un sentiment puissant, qui pénètre la nature extérieure, l'anime de sa même vie et la colore de sa teinte (CHH, t.VIII, p.206).

But this is still a long way from the doctrine of impersonality as he repeatedly defines it in his letters while he is working on *Madame Bovary*, and it appears that the formation of the final doctrine only took place in the wake of the criticisms of *La Tentation* so forcibly expressed by Bouilhet and Du Camp. Although *La Tentation* could hardly be described as directly autobiographical, it is self-indulgent, in that the author constantly gives in to the temptation of out-pourings of lyricism that are not justified by the exigencies of the work's structure. Certainly, Flaubert came to feel that he had been all too present in *La Tentation*: 'J'ai été moi-même dans *Saint Antoine* le saint et je l'ai oublié' (Corr., t.II, p.40), 'A la place de *Saint Antoine*, par exemple, c'est moi qui y suis: la tentation a été pour moi et non pour le lecteur' (Corr., t.II, p.127), 'C'était un déversoir; je n'ai eu que plaisir à l'écrire' (Corr., t.II, p.297).

Consequently, when he set about writing *Madame Bovary*, he was intensely aware of the need to avoid the traps into which he had fallen in *La Tentation*. 'Je veux qu'il n'y ait pas dans mon livre *un seul* mouvement, ni *une seule* réflexion de l'auteur. – Je crois que ce sera moins élevé que *Saint Antoine* comme *idées* (chose dont je fais peu de cas), mais ce sera peut-être plus raide et plus rare, sans qu'il y paraisse' (Corr., t.II, p.43). A few days later, he returns to the same idea: 'Ce sera diamétralement l'antipode de *Saint Antoine*, mais je crois que le style sera d'un art plus profond' (Corr., t.II, p. 46). But while the theory of impersonality may in part have evolved as a way of ensuring that he did not repeat the mistakes of *La Tentation*, there is much more to it than that. One important aspect is already adumbrated in the 1845 *Education*, when he summarises thus Jules's intentions:

> De même que le poète, en même temps qu'il est poète, doit être homme, c'est-à-dire résumer l'humanité dans son cœur et en être une portion quelconque, il demandait à l'œuvre d'art sa signification générale en même temps que sa valeur plastique et intrinsèque. [...] Dès lors, à travers le costume, l'époque, le pays, il cherchait l'homme: dans l'homme il cherchait le cœur' (CHH, t.VIII, p.208).

In other words, he was interested in a general human truth much more than in the particular truths of a given time and place. It is for that reason that the subtitle 'Mœurs de province' is misleading and that Flaubert could be so furious with critics who thought his concern was with 'observations de mœurs'. Obviously, the necessities of the novel form meant that he was obliged to deal with such particular truths, and he did so with fanatical conscientiousness, as is shown by his preoccupation with documentation and factual accuracy. Unlike Balzac or Zola, Flaubert never thought it the business of the novel to inform its readers about the workings of any given institution or sector of society, and in so far as his novels may in fact have done so, that was no more than an incidental side-effect.

Connected with this desire for a truth of generality is Flaubert's refusal to depict that which he regarded as exceptional or accidental. This is the explanation for what may seem the major paradox of his career as a novelist: despite the fact that art was the central pillar of his existence, after the perhaps half-hearted attempt of the first *Education*, he never showed the slightest inclination to write the novel of an artistic vocation.[58] The main reason for this abstention is no doubt the conviction that his own vocation, like his nervous illness, was a solitary accident, without universal human validity. 'Le premier venu est plus intéressant que M. Gustave Flaubert, parce que plus général et par conséquent plus typique' (Corr., t.III, p.575), and 'L'Art n'est pas fait pour peindre les exceptions' (Corr., t.III, p.575). Associated with this concern for a generally valid human truth is the feeling, which most of us share, that the more one is emotionally involved in a situation, the less likely one is to be able to view it objectively and to see what is really at issue in it: '*moins on sent une chose, plus on est apte à l'exprimer comme elle est*' (Corr., t.II, p.127). It follows from this that confessional literature, in which an author seeks to air or solve his personal problems, is necessarily an inferior and contaminated art form: 'rien de plus faible que de mettre en art ses sentiments personnels' (Corr., t.II, p.60); 'l'Art doit s'élever au-dessus des affections personnelles et des susceptibilités nerveuses' (Corr., t.II, p.691); 'je ne veux pas considérer l'Art comme un déversoir à passion' (Corr., t.II, p.557).

All these considerations undoubtedly play a part in the formation of Flaubert's doctrine of impersonality. But at the same time they are secondary. In spite of what might appear to be the logical sequence, it is less a matter of being impersonal in order to write better but to write well in order to be impersonal. The basic impulse behind all this is hatred of himself, and the hope of losing his own personality in art: '*pour ne pas vivre*, je me plonge dans l'Art, en désespéré' (Corr., t.III, p.65); 'la vie est une chose tellement hideuse que le seul moyen de la supporter est de l'éviter. Et on l'évite en vivant dans l'Art' (Corr., t.II, p.717); 'le seul moyen de supporter l'existence, c'est de s'étourdir dans la littérature comme dans une orgie perpétuelle' (Corr., t.II, p.832). Such declarations abound in his correspondence, and connect directly with other features of his behaviour. One such is his well-known dislike of images of himself: there are remarkably few photographs and portraits of Gustave Flaubert, obviously because he was extremely reluctant to have his likeness fixed and captured. Another is his unexpected confession one evening as Edmond de Goncourt accompanied him to the railway station: 'accoudé sur la traverse où on fait queue pour prendre les billets, il me parle de son profond ennui, de son aspiration à être mort – et mort sans métempsychose, sans survie, sans résurrection, à être à tout jamais depouillé de son moi'.[59] As he wrote to the unhappy Mademoiselle Leroyer de Chantepie not long after the publication of *Madame Bovary*, 'écrire l'histoire d'une autre. L'analyse d'une individualité étrangère vous écarterait de la vôtre' (Corr., t.III, p.26). There is no doubt that momentarily being Emma, or Charles, or Rodolphe, was for him the most effective way of forgetting the burden of being Gustave Flaubert.

But there is one vital point which must be remembered, though it is often neglected in discussions of Flaubert's doctrine of impersonality. That is that he never at any time fell victim to the illusion, fostered later by Zola, that the novelist could actually be absent from his creation and have no more control over it than the scientist has over the outcome of an experiment. What Flaubert aimed at was the illusion of impersonality, the appearance of the writer being so far as possible eliminated from the text. Hence the banishment of overt expressions of approval or disapproval or the insertion of disquisitions on moral, political or other issues, the avoidance of any explicit authorial comment on the events recounted or on the way in which they are presented. Flaubert was always keenly aware that the author was in fact responsible for everything that figured in his text, that every action, every detail implied a choice. Having Emma commit suicide rather than live happily ever after is already an option, an implicit expression of a view of the world. What Flaubert was intent on extirpating was any open expression of opinion which would betray the presence of the author. Clearly he had opinions, and vehement ones at that, and there could be no question of pretending otherwise. As he was to say many years later (but the principle is already wholly valid at the time of *Madame Bovary*): 'Je ne crois pas que le romancier doive exprimer *son* opinion sur les choses de ce monde. Il peut la communiquer, mais je n'aime pas à ce qu'il la dise. (Cela fait partie de ma poétique à moi). Je me borne donc à exposer les choses telles qu'elles me paraissent, à exprimer ce qui me semble être le vrai' (Corr., t.III, p.786). People, events, emotions will be set forth without comment, as though they were real 'facts', and it will be the reader's responsibility to draw any conclusions which might be indirectly suggested.

An example will help to clarify what Flaubert has in mind. We may take the description of the Abbé Bournisien as Emma visits him in the vain hope of receiving spiritual solace in her distress. This is how Flaubert depicts the priest as he emerges from the presbytery:

> Il fourra le catéchisme dans sa poche et s'arrêta, continuant à balancer entre deux doigts la lourde clef de la sacristie.
> La lueur du soleil couchant qui frappait en plein son visage pâlissait le lasting de sa soutane, luisante sous les coudes, effiloquée par le bas. Des taches de graisse et de tabac suivaient sur sa poitrine large la ligne des petits boutons, et elles devenaient plus nombreuses en s'écartant de son rabat, où reposaient les plis abondants de sa peau rouge; elle était semée de macules jaunes qui disparaissaient dans les poils rudes de sa barbe grisonnante. Il venait de dîner et respirait bruyamment (pp.114–115).

On the face of it, there is not a word of opinion, let alone of criticism, in this portrait of the priest. The unwary reader is led to suppose that Flaubert has no option but to portray him in this way, because that is how he is. But of course this is an illusion. There is no Abbé Bournisien, and Flaubert has imagined him in this way in order to say these things about him. In the nature of things, there must have been in the Normandy of the 1840s at least as many pale, lean and ascetic-looking country priests as there were who were stout, robust, red-faced and ill-kempt. Then one realises that the details of the description are carefully selected so as to create the impression of a gross physical presence with no sensitivity to anything non-physical – the use of the word 'fourra' rather than the neutral 'mit' implies casual indifference, as does the twirling of the key, the heaviness of which is brought out. The sunlight, that ethereal element, is obstructed by his face, and his robe is stained by the evidence of physical indulgence in snuff and greasy food. His double chin, red with yellow liver spots, disappears in the bristles of his beard, which are 'rudes' rather than 'fins', which would have been equally likely. And there is no reason in the logic of the narration why Emma's visit should take place immediately after dinner. Clearly, Flaubert has arranged matters in this way so as to be able to conclude his portrait with the climactic proof of Bournisien's coarseness: he has just finished a heavy meal and 'respirait bruyamment'. Flaubert's art has been to suggest that the picture of the priest is totally objective while contriving to prejudice any unsophisticated reader against him. Anyone alive to the unspoken implications of this passage must have begun to suspect that Bournisien is the last person in the world capable of dispensing spiritual comfort to Emma. Their subsequent conversation becomes ever more caricatural until Emma imploringly says to him: 'Oui [...] vous soulagez toutes les misères', and he replies : 'Ah! ne m'en parlez pas, Madame Bovary! Ce matin même il a fallu que j'aille dans le Bas-Diauville pour une vache qui avait l'*enfle*' (p.116). By this perhaps over-obvious device, Emma's sorrows and her immaterial longings are reduced to the status of 'une vache qui avait l'*enfle*'.

Of course, notwithstanding Flaubert's protestations, he does not always manage to remove himself so skilfully from the text. From time to time, the narrator intervenes openly to tell us something of which the characters are unaware: of Emma, 'elle ne savait pas que...' (p.103), or of Rodolphe: 'il ne distinguait pas...' (p.196). In addition *Madame Bovary* contains many aphorisms and generalisations, as D.A. Williams has pointed out.[60] But here there is a difficulty, deliberately created by Flaubert. When he writes, with reference to Emma's growing disillusionment with her lover: 'Il ne faut pas toucher aux idoles: la dorure en reste aux mains' (p.288), to whom are we to attribute this reflection? Is it something which is dawning on Emma? Is it an expository intervention by the narrator? Or is it simply part of the *doxa*, something which we all instinctively know to be true, perhaps without having explicitly formulated it? In some cases, the context may supply the answer, but in many others the ambiguity is unresolvable. One should notice too how often Flaubert smuggles in generalisations, by pretending that we all already know the point at issue. This is done by the formulation: 'one of those [...] which [...]'. For instance, referring to Rodolphe after his abandonment of Emma, he writes:

'Depuis trois ans, il l'avait soigneusement évitée par suite de cette lâcheté naturelle qui caractérise le sexe fort' (p.316), as though it was common knowledge that the supposedly stronger sex is characterised by natural cowardice. But many of us know no such thing and may not even agree that it is true. Further discussion of such techniques properly belongs to the analysis of Flaubert's use of 'style indirect libre' and as such will be postponed to the chapter devoted to that topic.

What it is important to see at this stage is how subtly Flaubert influences and manipulates the reactions of his readers and to understand what he meant by impersonality and what that idea did not encompass. One obvious consequence of the apparent elimination of the persona of the novelist is that the reader must not be reminded of the presence of an omniscient narrator pulling the strings and commenting on the action. Hence the pretence that the reader is in direct contact with the characters without the intermediary of a guide or instructor. Moralising comments will be eschewed: the reader will not be taken into the novelist's confidence over questions of plan and structure; in normal circumstances there will be no looking ahead to future events known to the narrator but not to the reader (though there are in *Madame Bovary* occasional infractions to this rule).[61] All this is in very conscious reaction against Balzac in particular, who is forever plucking his reader by the sleeve and giving him the benefit of his views on politics, morality, economics or whatever, who is telling him how he ought to distribute moral praise and blame on the characters, who is explaining why it is necessary to go back in time before embarking on the main story and so forth.

Of all Flaubert's contributions to the evolution of the novel, probably none has had a more intense and more durable impact than his cult of impersonality. In the eighteenth century, many novelists felt obliged, at least nominally, to establish the authenticity of their stories by more or less transparent devices: the collections of letters fortuitously assembled, the pseudo-memoirs, or the manuscript found in a trunk. Once these devices had worn threadbare, the narrator's guarantee came to be seen as sufficient. But that assumption of authority by the narrator in itself led to the narrator taking on a more and more prominent position in the forefront of the work, judging the behaviour of the characters, overtly conditioning the reader's responses, even confiding in him the problems of the narration. Before Flaubert's time, it was thus almost inevitable that the reader would constantly be reminded that he was reading a novel. Flaubert's aim in *Madame Bovary* was to make the reader forget that a man called Gustave Flaubert had written a novel entitled *Madame Bovary* and to make him think for the duration of his reading that he was in direct contact with Emma Bovary, Charles Bovary, Rodolphe Boulanger and the others. This aim was naturally supported by extremely high standards of verisimilitude, documentary observation and the like. All this was avidly seized on by Zola and his disciples, who tended to interpret it in a way which Flaubert himself vigorously rejected, since he, unlike some of his successors, never lost sight of the fact that, in the last analysis, a novel is the product of essentially subjective options: 'l'Art n'est pas la nature [...] on est obligé de choisir', as he was to write many years later to Huysmans (CHH., t.XVI, p.160). Not for him Zola's hasty assimilation of the novelist to a species of scientist. When Flaubert compares the novelist to a scientist (as he does from time to time), he means no more than that the novelist must work with the same detachment and impartiality as a scientist. But the Realist-Naturalist view of the novel which tended to hold sway for three or four decades in the latter half of the nineteenth century itself left a lasting legacy, even when new generations such as that of Proust and Gide had turned to the view of the novel as an autonomous genre which was betraying its own specificity if it pretended to be something else. But while in the twentieth century new novel forms came to the fore, the fact remains that a high proportion of modern novel production, whether or not it lays claim to literary excellence, still tends to conform to the Flaubertian ideal of a story which tells itself, effacing the presence and visible guiding hand of the author.

There is one way in which the reader can be reminded of the presence of a narrator and that is by the insertion of images which would not naturally occur to any of the characters. Unlike most people, Flaubert had a spontaneously florid style which Du Camp and Bouilhet felt had run riot in the first *Tentation*, so the writer was well aware of the dangers and the need to exercise restraint. But this was a task he did not find easy, and in 1852 he wrote to Louise Colet: 'Je suis gêné par le sens métaphorique qui décidément me domine trop. Je suis dévoré de comparaisons comme on l'est de poux, et je ne passe mon temps qu'à les écraser, mes phrases en grouillent' (Corr., t.II, p.220). In later novels, Flaubert has mastered the discipline of controlling the exuberance of his imagery, but in *Madame Bovary* there are places where his pen tends to run away with him. One thinks in particular of the elaborate image of Emma trying to keep alive her love for Léon, like a traveller in the steppes of Russia striving to preserve some warmth in the embers of his dying fire (pp.127–128).[62] But if this is the most brilliant and self-conscious of the images in *Madame Bovary*, Flaubert himself had doubts about its appropriateness: 'Je viens de sortir d'une *comparaison soutenue* qui a d'étendue près de deux pages. C'est un morceau, comme on dit, ou du moins je le crois. Mais peut-être est-ce trop pompeux pour la couleur générale du livre, et me faudra-t-il plus tard le retrancher' (Corr., t.II, p.351). If in the end he allowed it to stand, it is probably because it does not seem out of place in the overall colouring of the imagery in the novel. Don Demorest, in his monumental study of Flaubert's imagery, makes the point firmly: 'Les formes les plus travaillées mais les plus fortes des images dominent bien plus dans ce roman que dans le reste de Flaubert, ce qui indique à quel point il les a soignées'.[63] Certainly, beside the striking imagery of *Madame Bovary*, the style of the 1869 *Education sentimentale*, where one would be hard put to it to find a single comparison that might be called poetic, can seem flat and uninteresting, and that is no doubt one of the reasons for the relative unpopularity of the later novel. This flatness is of course a matter of deliberate policy, but it also indicates that Flaubert in the meantime has acquired greater control and greater discretion in the handling of images. As Demorest admits, in *Madame Bovary* 'quelques-unes [des images] ont l'inconvénient de ne pas s'accorder très bien avec le credo de l'effacement de l'auteur dans son œuvre'.[64] Of course, the resources of 'style indirect libre', which we shall be examining later, enable him in many cases to leave it open whether images originate in the feelings of the characters or in the mind of the artist. But one has to recognise that, for better or for worse, the images in *Madame Bovary* draw attention to themselves much more than in any other of his mature novels.

But even allowing for the number of concealed expressions of opinion and the giveaway brilliance of some of the images, it is incontrovertible that *Madame Bovary* is the first novel in which the author systematically sets out to efface, so far as possible, all traces of his presence, thereby inaugurating a convention which governed most fiction, especially in France, for the next forty years and which still rules in most non-experimental novels today.

V Point of view

Obviously, one of the most evident ways in which the authorial presence shows itself is through the conveying of information to which only an omniscient narrator could be privy. The case of Balzac is again illuminating. In the early pages of most Balzac novels, we are supplied with the past history of the protagonists, with details of their present situation and relationships, and with a full portrait of their dress, appearance and habitat. Since all this can only come from an omniscient narrator, his presence is clear and undisguised. Such a technique is repugnant to Flaubert, since it constitutes a slight but unmistakable infraction of the code of impersonality. To obviate this inconvenience, Flaubert prefers to shelter behind one or other of the characters in the novel and to provide only such information as he or she might possess or notice. So it is that *Madame Bovary* begins with the words: 'Nous étions à l'Etude...' (p.3), implying that what we are about to read will be recounted from the point of view of one of Charles's schoolfellows. In the event, this proves not to be the case, since very soon we are being told all manner of things which no school-fellow of Charles could possibly have known. Many commentators on the novel have been perplexed by this anomaly, and we shall have occasion to study the reasons for Flaubert's having proceeded in this way. But it is sufficient for the moment to note that it avoids the necessity for launching into the narrative under the authority of an omniscient and extradiegetic narrator.

A more typical example of the use of point of view comes when Charles pays his first visit to Les Bertaux to attend to Rouault's broken leg. As he nears the farm, he is met by a boy who is to show him the way: 'L'officier de santé, chemin faisant, comprit aux discours de son guide que M. Rouault était un cultivateur des plus aisés. Il s'était cassé la jambe, la veille au soir, en revenant de *faire les Rois* chez un voisin. Sa femme était morte depuis deux ans. Il n'avait avec lui que sa *demoiselle*, qui l'aidait à tenir la maison' (p.14).

So we know exactly as much about Rouault as Charles does, and no more, and we discover it entirely through Charles's experience. (In fact, some of the information supplied by the boy turns out to be wrong: far from being prosperous, Rouault is a bad farmer who loses money every year). As they enter the farm itself, 'son cheval eut peur et fit un grand écart' (p.15). Presented as a factual statement by the narrator, it is up to the reader to decide, with nothing to direct his response, whether this is a pure meaningless accident or some sort of warning of fate. We then see the farm buildings as Charles sees them: stables with horses inside, heaps of manure with hens and turkeys pecking at them, a high barn, a shed containing carts and ploughs, a farmyard surrounded by trees, and a noisy flock of geese by the pond. A young woman wearing a blue woollen dress ushers him indoors to the kitchen with its dishes cooking on the fire, its damp clothing set out to dry, pots and pans gleaming in the firelight. After visiting the injured man, Charles returns to the kitchen with the young woman, who, while sewing, pricks her fingers 'qu'elle portait ensuite à sa bouche pour les sucer' (p.16). Charles is surprised by the whiteness of her fingernails but registers the fact that her hand is too long and rather bony, and that she has fine dark eyes. In the course of the scene, we hear of her rather full lips, her black hair parted in the middle, her pink cheeks and her horn-rimmed spectacles fastened to her dress. That is, for the time being, all we are told about her, and we infer that it may be all Charles notices. The contrast with what Balzac would have done in similar circumstances is extraordinary. When a major character makes his first appearance in a novel of the *Comédie humaine*, Balzac almost invariably treats the reader to an exhaustive description of him or her: height, corpulence, hair-colour, shape of face, demeanour, complexion, any physical peculiarities, detail of dress and so on, whether or not there is anyone there to notice such things, very often accompanying the description with interpretative comments designed to allow us to make deductions about the inner psychology from the outward appearance. There is nothing of this sort about our (and Charles's) introduction to Emma, and not much is added in the course of the novel to the meagre details we are given about her physique.

Illustrating a Balzac novel is a relatively easy task because the author has taken so much trouble to allow us to envisage the character in the minutest of his or her outer characteristics. We shall return later to the function of description in *Madame Bovary*, but it is already apparent that Flaubert wishes to leave a sufficient margin of vagueness and imprecision in his evocation of Emma (and the others) for each reader to construct his own image of her. It is open to the reader to see in the gesture of her sucking her fingers an indication of her sensuality, but nothing is specified to force us to reach that conclusion, any more than the imperceptive Charles is able to.

Readers have occasionally been surprised that Flaubert chose to begin *Madame Bovary* from Charles's point of view, after the initial introduction from that of one of his classmates, but, as we shall see, he had excellent and multiple reasons for doing so. Once he has adopted the point of view of Charles, Flaubert very largely keeps to it until Chapter IV, when he shifts to that of Emma. Thereafter it is Emma's perspective which predominates until her death. But even in this central portion of the novel, Flaubert varies the angle of vision: sometimes we return to Charles's point of view, sometimes we see things through the eyes of Léon or Rodolphe, when it is necessary for us to be acquainted with things of which Emma is unaware, such as Léon's mute adoration or Rodolphe's treachery. There is even a momentary transfer to the perspective of minor characters, when Mesdames Caron and Tuvache observe from a distance Emma's visit to Binet when she is desperately seeking money to stave off the final catastrophe. It is at all events very rare, save for brief passages, for there to be no one to witness or experience what is happening. However, there is one notable exception to this, and that is the evocation of Yonville when Charles and Emma move there at the beginning of Part Two. There, for several pages, it is an impersonal narrator who is charged with the task of informing the reader of the history, topography and economy of the village, and many critics have commented, sometimes adversely,[65] on this seeming reversion to a Balzacian technique. But Flaubert is justified in departing from his usual practice in this case. One reason is that Part One of the

51

novel is by way of being a prologue to the real action, which only engages when the Bovarys are in Yonville. Flaubert thus needs to give a full account of the setting, which he could not do if he were to split up his evocation of the village among the perceptions of several different characters. More importantly, since it is the atmosphere of Yonville which will ultimately suffocate and destroy Emma, he wants to present it as a coherent whole. It would be much less stifling if it were divided and compartmentalised; as it is, there are no interstices through which Emma might escape.

The other main occasion on which Flaubert forsakes the point of view of a single character is the famous cab-ride round Rouen during which Emma becomes Léon's mistress. No one follows or could conceivably follow the cab's capricious itinerary: 'On la vit à...' (pp.249–250) a whole jumbled list of quarters and suburbs of Rouen, and the reader briefly shares the cab-driver's puzzlement. But of course, as is so often the case, the intelligent reader understands much more than he is explicitly told. The reasons for this recourse to the point of view of the anonymous citizenry are not hard to discern. There are three decisive sexual encounters in Emma's life: her wedding-night with Charles, her seduction by Rodolphe, and her becoming Léon's mistress. Clearly decency forbade any account of them from the point of view of the participants, so Flaubert was obliged to resort to three different devices to circumvent the difficulty. The wedding-night was easily resolved: the recital of the events of the wedding is largely seen from the point of view of the guests, so attention could be concentrated on their activities without any need to violate the privacy of the newly-weds' bedroom. It is only the next morning that Flaubert drops a hint about how things had gone: 'C'est plutôt lui que l'on eût pris pour la vierge de la veille, tandis que la mariée ne laissait rien découvrir où l'on pût deviner quelque chose' (p.31). The contrast between Charles's blushes and Emma's self-possession is expressive of the difference in their character and the intensity of their relative pleasure. With the seduction scene in the forest, Flaubert makes use of a device which was to become a commonplace of film directors. At the moment when the sexual act is consummated, the focus moves from the lovers to their surroundings: 'elle s'abandonna. / Les ombres du soir descendaient; le soleil horizontal, passant entre les branches, lui éblouissait les yeux' (p.165). For Léon, Flaubert clearly wanted a contrast with the open-air roughness of the affair with Rodolphe and adopts, without undue care for verisimilitude (but that is another story), the solution of the cab-ride, where, as with the wedding-night, the reader can safely be left to imagine what is happening inside the enclosed space.

In addition to helping to disguise the presence and organising activity of a narrator, the technique of multiple viewpoints has several other advantages. One is ensuring that all, or nearly all, the characters have an inner life with which we are made to sympathise. We may despise Rodolphe for his heartless philandering, but we cannot help but share in his feelings (or lack of feelings) towards Emma. Another is the production of unspoken drama through the juxtaposition of two conflicting points of view. Perhaps the most striking example occurs after the disastrous failure of the operation on Hippolyte's club foot, when Charles and Emma, side by side, pursue their divergent reflections: 'Il avait pris pourtant toutes les précautions imaginables. La fatalité s'en était mêlée [...]. Comment donc avait-elle fait (elle qui était si intelligente!) pour se méprendre encore une fois? Du reste, par quelle déplorable manie avoir ainsi abîmé son existence en sacrifices continuels?' (p.189). The reader is well aware of the self-delusion each is practising: clearly Fate is no more responsible for Hippolyte's misfortune than Emma's unhappiness is a consequence of her supposed sacrifices. The drama of the situation is no les poignant for being unspoken: the only words uttered are Emma's 'Assieds-toi, tu m'agaces!' (p.189) and Charles's pathetic question: 'Mais c'était peut-être un valgus?' (p.190). Yet another overtone produced by the technique is that of the inevitable relativity of perceptions. Emma and Charles are both reacting to the same event, but while both have perhaps some justification, both are wrong, and the narrator is careful to abstain from arbitrating between them.

Henry James was critical of Flaubert's choice of Emma (and later of Frédéric Moreau in *L'Education sentimentale*) as the central character through whom most of the action is perceived: 'Our complaint is that Emma Bovary, in spite of her consciousness and in spite of reflecting so much that of her creator, is really too small an affair. [...] Why did Flaubert choose, as special conduits of the life he proposed to depict, such inferior and in the case of Frédéric such abject human specimens?'[66] Admittedly, James's strictures apply much more forcibly to Frédéric, and it is also true that in *L'Education sentimentale*, Frédéric's perspective dominates much more than Emma's does in *Madame Bovary*. But in any case it is false to argue that the reader is limited to Emma's responses and perceptions. He can make all sorts of corrections to her views and emotions and is constantly incited to do so, both by the changes to the point of view of other characters, so that we know much more about Charles, Léon and Rodolphe than she ever could, and by the omnipresent irony which underpins so much of what she thinks or feels, and which is so unobtrusively conveyed by a telltale word or a change of sentence rhythm. This happens for instance when she is going through her religious phase on recovering from the illness provoked by Rodolphe's precipitate departure: 'Elle entrevit, parmi les illusions de son espoir, un état de pureté flottant au-dessus de la terre, se confondant avec le ciel, et où elle aspira d'être. Elle voulut devenir une sainte' (p.219). The term 'illusions' alerts the reader to the falsity of her dreams and visions, and the sudden descent from the sustained phrases of the first sentence to the brutal concision of the second makes him see how absurd it is for Emma (or perhaps anyone) to decide that it would be pleasant to accede to sainthood. While it is essential that we are made to sympathise with Emma's aspirations, it is equally essential that we should not be duped by them. There is thus no question of our reactions being limited by those of Emma.

One curious effect of this point-of-view technique is the occasional discrepancy which arises between what are presented as the 'objective' facts about a person and the 'subjective' vision which we as readers form about that person as a result of continually seeing him with Emma's eyes. This is no doubt most apparent in the case of Charles. What is stated as 'fact' about him is not particularly discreditable: he is not bad-looking, he is devoted to Emma, he is not unduly incompetent as a doctor, he is not rancorous. Yet it is difficult for us not to think of him as clumsy, unimaginative, stupid and mediocre, because that is how Emma sees him. This contrast between the 'objective' statements and the 'subjective' view presents real problems for a dramatic or cinematic adaptation of *Madame Bovary*, and in at least two film versions of the novel, Vincente Minnelli's in 1949 and Claude Chabrol's in 1991, the actor playing the part of Charles (Van Heflin for Minnelli[67] and Jean-François Balmer for Chabrol) comes across as a much more sympathetic figure than he does from a reading of the text. The spectator feels a pity for him in his misfortunes which the reader is unlikely to (at least until the closing chapters). In both cases, he has of course his visible shortcomings: he is excessively docile, he is blind to his wife's feelings and to her infidelities, he overreaches himself ridiculously when he attempts a complicated operation on Hippolyte's club foot. But, as R.J. Sherrington has pointed out,[68] in the episode of the visit to the textile mill, there is a highly prejudicial picture of Charles: 'Il avait sa casquette enfoncée sur les sourcils, et ses deux grosses lèvres tremblotaient, ce qui ajoutait à son visage quelque chose de stupide; son dos même, son dos tranquille était irritant à voir, et elle y trouvait étalée sur la redingote toute la platitude du personnage' (p.104). Only Emma could be irritated by his rear view, and only she could find 'toute la platitude du personnage' on the back of his overcoat, or make his lips indicate semi-imbecility. Yet the reader finds himself sharing her feelings of frustrated revulsion, whether or not there is any real justification for them. Here as elsewhere a little reflection makes one realise that there is no single univocal truth: Charles is in essence unexceptionable but he is also extremely irritating, and it would certainly be wrong to maintain that one of these perceptions is right and the other not. As Flaubert was to write not long before his death (but the idea had been with him for years): 'Il n'y a pas de vrai! Il n'y a que des manières de voir' (CHH, t.XVI, p.308). The multiplicity of perspectives in *Madame Bovary* reflects in practice this notion of the relativity of truth.

VI   Dialogue and 'style indirect libre'[69]

Inseparable from the question of point of view in *Madame Bovary* is the analysis of one of Flaubert's most celebrated and most discussed innovations, the consistent use of what is usually termed 'style indirect libre', that is to say, the introduction of passages, sentences or phrases of reported speech, usually in the imperfect but sometimes in the present tense but without specific indication of the origin of the speech, thought or feelings. It is thus often the reader's responsibility to decide whether what is reported should be attributed to one of the characters, to the narrator or to generally accepted opinion. In many cases there can be no hesitation, but in others the ambiguity is total and unresolvable. As with point of view, the use of 'style indirect libre' is a valuable means of masking the presence of the author, but it has other advantages too, which cannot be dissociated from the general problem of dialogue in *Madame Bovary*. It will therefore be convenient to begin by examining Flaubert's attitude to dialogue at the time of embarking on *Madame Bovary*.

By 1851, Flaubert had considerable experience in the handling of dialogue, from his numerous dramatic experiments and from his prose stories. He had often aimed at picturesqueness: in *Loys XI*, for example, there is a good deal of pseudo-medievalism, and in some of the tales he is clearly concerned to reproduce idio-syncratic speech patterns, the more so as he adored imitating people: Maxime Du Camp tells us that he was so pleased with his imitation of the famous actress Marie Dorval that for weeks he constantly spoke with her intonations and peculiarities,[70] and we know that throughout his life he delighted in copying the speech mannerisms of imaginary or real models, from Napoleon III to Norman peasants.[71] With this background and with the massive precedent of Balzac and his careful mimicking of dialect and accent, most notoriously the Alsatian pronunciation of Baron Nucingen, one might think that Flaubert would have relished the prospect of reproducing the oral characteristics of his varied cast of characters in *Madame Bovary*. But in fact this was not the case at all, and he was greatly exercised by the difficulty of handling dialogue in his novel.

The problem stemmed from the conflict between giving a reasonable approximation to real speech and maintaining a sufficient elevation of style. One of the people whom Flaubert most enjoyed imitating was the actor and playwright Henry Monnier, particularly in his invented persona of Joseph Prud-homme, the sententious, philistine bourgeois. In his day, Monnier had the reputation of being the *nec plus ultra* in the reproduction of everyday conversation, with its clichés, its incoherences and its lack of true expressivity. But however much Flaubert may have admired Monnier and appreciated his ability to recreate the features of everyday discourse, this was precisely what worried him about the integration of dialogue in *Madame Bovary*. Having against all his inclinations been persuaded of the necessity for taking a contemporary subject from ordinary life, Flaubert was well aware that it would be wildly inappropriate to endow his characters with any sort of eloquence in their speech. On the other hand, he was convinced that the sordid nature of the subject could only be redeemed by conferring on the language a level of literary excellence. In September 1852, he wrote to Louise Colet: 'Ce que j'écris présentement risque d'être du Paul de Kock si je n'y mets une forme profondément littéraire', only to sigh anxiously: 'Mais comment faire du dialogue trivial qui soit bien écrit?' (Corr., t.II, p.156). Formulated in these terms, the dilemma seems almost insoluble.

One obvious tactic which Flaubert naturally adopts is a drastic reduction in the amount of dialogue in the novel compared with his predecessors. Claudine Gothot-Mersch has calculated that in a novel like *La Cousine Bette* almost half the text consists of directly reported dialogue.[72] The proportion in *Madame Bovary* is no more than 20%. Balzac loves organising scenes of dramatic conflict in which two or more characters exchange longer or shorter speeches heavily charged with emotion. But for Flaubert language generally is a collection of stereotyped formulae in which we all, willy-nilly, are forced to repeat commonplaces which bear little relationship to the individuality of our feelings and intentions. We shall see later some remarkable illustrations of this lack of faith in the expressive quality of language as it is used in an everyday context. It is well-known that, throughout nearly all of his active career, one of Flaubert's most cherished projects was the *Dictionnaire des idées reçues*, which at the time of his death he was polishing for inclusion in the second volume of *Bouvard et Pécuchet*, and that he was obsessed by the extent to which any statement, both in form and content, is of necessity a repetition. This being so, the possibility of meaningful dramatic dialogue in the Balzacian sense is drastically reduced. If one analyses almost any of the dialogue scenes in *Madame Bovary* – the conversation between Emma and Léon at the Lion d'or, the verbal seduction of Emma by Rodolphe at the Comices – one sees that there is little real communication between the participants (though in the latter case the sense of mutual attraction comes through clearly enough). Each utters platitudes and idiocies that hardly connect with their innermost emotions, and the responses are equally remote from anything that might be called sincerity. This is one of the reasons for Flaubert's lack of success as a dramatist; whereas Monnier in his playlets exaggerates the inconsequentiality and insipidity of normal conversation to the point where it becomes absurd, hence comic, Flaubert keeps closer to an observed reality so that the dialogue of his plays can seem flat and prolix without being amusing.

But even if Flaubert consciously reduces the amount of direct dialogue in *Madame Bovary*, that does not mean that he is dispensed from recording what passes verbally between the characters, however hackneyed it may be. As he complains to Louise Colet in 1853: 'Peindre par le dialogue et qu'il ne soit pas moins vif, précis et toujours distingué en restant même banal, cela est monstrueux, et je ne sache personne qui l'ait fait dans un livre' (Corr., t.II, p.444). This is where and why the role of 'style indirect libre' is crucial. In the first place, it reduces the disparity, which so worried Flaubert, between the literary quality of his narratorial prose and the banality of reported conversation, since, instead of reproducing the incoherence of real dialogue, he can convert what is thought or said into his own words and integrate it into the flow of the narrative, so long as he does not depart too visibly from the limited expressive capacities of his characters. Secondly, he can obscure the frontier between a character's words and his own, so that his presence is not readily detectable. There are innumerable possibilities of variation with this system, and a few examples will clarify this and demonstrate the remarkable virtuosity with which Flaubert manipulates it.

Here, for instance, is his description of Emma's dissatisfaction with Tostes: 'Une aventure amenait parfois des péripéties à l'infini, et le décor changeait. Mais, pour elle, rien n'arrivait, Dieu l'avait voulu! L'avenir était un corridor noir, et qui avait au fond sa porte bien fermée' (p.65). The first two sentences are clearly a straight-forward report of Emma's musings: her imagining of possible adventures, her frustration at the emptiness of her life, her putting the blame on God. But then the artist takes over and provides Emma with a metaphor which, while not lying outside her experience, is not represented as having specifically occurred to her (it is true, as we have seen with the image of the fire on the steppes, that Flaubert's penchant for striking imagery can lead him to overstep the mark and show his authorial hand too clearly). Here is another case, where, pursuing his aim of reserving direct dialogue for the more important scenes, he summarises a series of repetitive conversations between Emma, her neighbours and Charles about her diminishing pianistic capabilities: 'Et quand on venait la voir, elle ne manquait pas de vous apprendre qu'elle avait abandonné la musique et ne pouvait maintenant s'y remettre, pour des raisons majeures. Alors on la plaignait. C'était dommage! elle qui avait un si beau talent! On en parla même à Bovary. On lui faisait honte, et surtout le pharmacien' (p.266). The conversations would be of no great interest in themselves, and it would be pointless to specify the 'raisons majeures' to which Emma ascribes her abandonment of music, since they are inevitably false and specious. But something of the flavour of these exchanges is suggested by the interpolation, without explanation, of what are visibly the sort of remarks made by her friends: 'C'était dommage! elle qui avait un si beau talent!'. By these means, the rapidity of the narration is maintained in a seamless structure which nevertheless conveys the atmosphere of these conversations.

One exceptional case requires special consideration. This occurs in the latter stages of Emma's affair with Rodolphe, when he is beginning to tire of her cloying importunities. Flaubert begins by recording Emma's flattery of her lover: 'Je suis ta servante et ta concubine! Tu es mon roi, mon idole! tu es bon! tu es beau! tu es intelligent! tu es fort!' (p.196). By this string of exclamation marks not followed by capital letters, we are made to realise how thoughtlessly Emma is rattling out these tired old compliments. Following this, we have a sentence of narrative explanation: 'Il s'était tant de fois entendu dire ces choses qu'elles n'avaient pour lui rien d'original'. Then comes an observation of which it is hard to say whether it is narratorial commentary or Rodolphe's point of view: 'Emma ressemblait à toutes les maîtresses; et le charme de la nouveauté, peu à peu tombant comme un vêtement, laissait voir à nu l'éternelle monotonie de la passion qui a toujours les mêmes formes et le même langage'. Once again Flaubert has introduced an image, that of novelty disappearing like a dropped dress, so that, although we are following Rodolphe's reactions, the style benefits from a comparison which comes from within his range of experience but is unlikely to have occurred to someone so lacking in imagination. But one has the impression of a change of perspective at the end with the reference to 'la passion qui a toujours les mêmes formes et le même langage'. This is no doubt Rodolphe's opinion, but the present tense indicates that it is more than just that: either a truth which we all recognise or a view which the author shares with Rodolphe – certainly what comes next proves that, even if it is Rodolphe's idea, he is not wrong to hold it. But then we find a much more drastic change, when the introductory phrase makes it clear that we are now specifically departing from Rodolphe's point of view: 'Il ne distinguait pas, cet homme si plein de pratique, la dissemblance des sentiments sous la parité des expressions'. Following this switch, Flaubert waxes vehement in what is no doubt his most overt intervention in the novel:

Parce que des lèvres libertines ou vénales lui avaient murmuré des phrases pareilles, il ne croyait que faiblement à la candeur de celles-là: on en devait rabattre, pensait-il, les discours exagérés cachant les affections médiocres.

Nowhere else in *Madame Bovary* or possibly anywhere in Flaubert's novels would one find such an explicit condemnation of a mistake made by a character. The novelist's indignation then bursts out without disguise of any sort:

comme si la plénitude de l'âme ne débordait pas quelquefois par les métaphores les plus vides, puisque personne, jamais, ne peut donner l'exacte mesure de ses besoins, ni de ses conceptions, ni de ses douleurs, et que la parole humaine est comme un chaudron fêlé où nous battons des mélodies à faire danser les ours, quand on voudrait attendrir les étoiles.

In part, this is of course the permanently rankling resentment of the writer vainly struggling with the inadequacies of language, which we have already noted. But there is also, and more importantly, a particular point which Flaubert deems it imperative to make in *Madame Bovary*, even at the expense of a flagrant breach of his code of impersonality. This is to ensure that the reader does not fall into the same trap as Rodolphe, namely, assuming that because the forms Emma uses to express her longings and emotions are tawdry and secondhand, that these longings and emotions are themselves inauthentic. But the technique by which Flaubert departs so visibly from his normal practice is very revealing. He begins by insinuating the reader into Rodolphe's consciousness, then gradually alters the perspective until he is unmistakably and violently speaking in his own name. But unless the reader is alive to these subtle shifts, he may well not notice what has happened.

One inevitable consequence of converting dialogue into 'style indirect libre' is a certain flattening of the tone (except for the insertion of images). Flaubert does not show the same interest as Balzac in recording picturesque speech variations, such as dialect, slang or pronunciation. In *Madame Bovary*, he gives a few features of popular or peasant syntax or vocabulary to minor characters, like old Rouault or Madame Lefrançois, and of course he endows Homais's speech with a great deal of platitudinous pomposity, but as Claudine Gothot-Mersch has observed,[73] the spoken language of the main characters is on the whole correct but neutral in tone. It seems to be with reluctance that Flaubert reproduces grammatical incorrections: Claudine Gothot-Mersch[74] and Sterling Haig[75] both pick up the same modification to the drafts as evidence of this scruple. In the draft of the scene of Charles's first visit to Les Bertaux, the boy who is sent to show him the way says: 'C'est-y vous qu'est le médecin?' which in the definitive text is altered to read: 'Etes-vous le médecin?' (p.14). Similarly, with reference to Rouault's letter to Emma and Charles, we are told: 'Les fautes d'orthographe s'y enlaçaient les unes aux autres' (p.177), but in the letter as it is reproduced, although the style is simple, with a solitary regional term ('*picots*' for 'dindons'), there is not a single spelling mistake, though in this case the spelling is equally orthodox in the drafts. It is true that in *Madame Bovary* Flaubert makes liberal use of italics, signalling normandisms (as with the 'picots' just quoted) or drawing attention to some turn of phrase which he evidently considers specially bourgeois. As Claude Duchet has put it: 'l'italique est une métaphore du sens et désigne la parole dévaluée du discours social: le roman s'y installe, en fait sa langue, mais en exhibant le fonctionnement autologique de ce discours, qui se parle lui-même, se ressasse et n'a rien à dire, si ce n'est la façon dont il assure la cohérence d'un texte et la cohésion d'une société'.[76] One has the impression that Flaubert fears that incorrect or stereotyped French may be attributed to him rather than to his characters or to the society of which they are part, and wishes to alert the reader to the fact that he accepts no personal responsibility for such deviations or banalities (in fact, there are quite a few Norman expressions, no doubt inadvertent, in the narratorial prose too). All these features tend to move Flaubert away from the sort of picturesqueness in which Balzac revels and represent a strategy radically different from that which Zola was to adopt in *L'Assommoir*, where the distinction between the popular language of the characters and the narrator's prose is effaced by allowing the popular idiom to invade the narrative as well as the dialogue.

Flaubert's combination of dialogue and 'style indirect libre' is one of his most original and influential techniques, and gives *Madame Bovary* a character all of its own, since what he does there is not something which he simply repeats in subsequent novels: the refusal to use striking imagery in *L'Education sentimentale*, the syntactic and lexical discontinuities of the later work are very different from the more highly coloured style of *Madame Bovary*: as he wrote while composing *L'Education*, 'pas de scène capitale, *pas de morceau*, pas même de métaphore, car la moindre broderie emporterait la trame' (Corr., t.III, p.600). It has been pointed out by George Pistorius[77] that in *Madame Bovary* all the characters, except Charles, employ comparisons, whereas there are no more than a dozen in all the dialogues of *L'Education*.

In his comments to others on the use of dialogue in the novel, Flaubert invariably insists that passages of direct speech should be reserved for important scenes. Here for example is what he wrote in 1858 to his friend Ernest Feydeau about the latter's novel *Daniel*: 'La partie faible du style, c'est le dialogue, *quand il n'est pas important du fond*. [...] Je ne dis pas de retrancher les idées, *mais d'adoucir comme ton* celles qui sont secondaires. Pour cela, il faut les reculer, c'est-à-dire les rendre plus courtes et les écrire au style indirect' (Corr., t.II, p.852). The same advice was offered in 1870 to Léon de Saint-Valéry, a budding novelist who had sought his counsel: 'Pourquoi ne pas vous servir plus souvent de la forme narrative et réserver le style direct pour les *scènes* principales?' (Corr., t.IV, p.155). Similarly in 1874 he criticised Zola for the same defect in *La Conquête de Plassans*: 'peut-être aussi y a-t-il un peu trop de dialogues, dans les parties accessoires' (CHH, t.XV, p.305). The principle seems clear and categorical, founded, for the reasons we have seen, on what the author himself describes as 'la haine que j'ai du dialogue dans les romans' (Corr., t.III, p.625). Yet Marie-Thérèse Mathet has argued that Flaubert is by no means consistent in his application of it in *Madame Bovary*.[78] Some potentially crucial scenes are completely elided: the discussion between Emma and her father which leads to the acceptance of

Charles's proposal of marriage or the attempt by Emma to persuade Binet to give her money. Equally Flaubert has a tendency to 'nous rapporter dans toute sa longueur et sa banalité l'ensemble d'une conversation parfaitement futile',[79] instancing the conversation between Emma and the wet-nurse when she visits her with Léon or the importunate chatter of the *suisse* to Emma and Léon in the cathedral. Beside that, there are of course several dialogue scenes which mark vital moments of the action or the structure of the novel: Charles's first day at school, the conversation at the Lion d'or when the Bovarys arrive in Yonville, or the various parts of the episode of the Comices. Some of these apparent inconsistencies are easily explained: the elision of Emma's discussion with her father makes us share the tension and impatience of Charles as he waits to hear his fate and means that we are not yet privileged to share in her emotions, just as the *suisse*'s rambling discourse heightens Léon's irritation and suspense. And eliding Emma's pleas to Binet avoids what would have been a doubling up with the similar but much more significant scenes when Emma goes to Guillaumin and subsequently to Rodolphe with the same request. But it would hardly be possible to account in this way for all the infringements of his own precept that one can detect in *Madame Bovary*.

It may well be that the explanation for these gaps between theory and practice resides in Flaubert's ambivalent attitude to language. He hates dialogue in the novel because he knows that most speech is platitudinous and conveys little of the real individual feelings of people. On the other hand, he is well aware that for most of us drama consists in violent verbal or physical confrontations and that a novel devoid of drama would be uninteresting almost to the point of unreadability (although he comes close to trying to realise such a concept in *L'Education sentimentale* and *Bouvard et Pécuchet*). As he wrote to Louise Colet in 1853, with reference to *Madame Bovary*: 'Le drame y a peu de part' (Corr., t.II, p.361), and a few weeks later, to the same correspondent he made a particularly revealing comment in connection with the Comices: 'J'arrive au dramatique rien que par l'entrelacement du dialogue et les oppositions de caractère' (Corr., t.II, p.449). This remark makes one wonder exactly what he understood by 'le dramatique'; given the context, it seems unlikely that he had in mind that which is terrible or tragic. It is more probable that he was thinking of that which would interest or involve the reader and in which dialogue was only one element among others. So he was evidently torn between two contradictory attitudes to dialogue: on the one hand, it was required for scenes of conflict and crisis, but on the other it served to reveal the inanity of language and the way in which people use it. Hence the co-existence of dialogue scenes which present critical events and others which hardly advance the action and concern only trivialities. There are even occasions when the two opposing functions occur simultaneously, as is the case with the Comices of which Flaubert writes: 'Dans ce moment-ci, par exemple, je viens de montrer dans un dialogue qui roule sur la pluie et le beau temps, un particulier qui doit être à la fois bon enfant, commun, un peu canaille et prétentieux! Et à travers tout cela, il faut qu'on voie qu'il *pousse sa pointe*' (Corr., t.II, p.445). So while it is clearly important for the progress of the action that Rodolphe is softening up Emma in preparation for his intended seduction, the fact that he is talking only of 'la pluie et le beau temps' indicates a desire to underline the irrelevance of the nominal subject of his discourse. This is in turn further suggested by Flaubert's intention of making the reader hear 'à la fois des beuglements de taureaux, des soupirs d'amour et des phrases d'administrateurs' (Corr., t.II, p.449), all of them ultimately just as meaningless.

Stirling Haig has provided a pertinent summing-up of dialogue in *Madame Bovary* and Flaubert's later novels: 'Dialogue in Flaubert seeks to portray not individual quirks, but to circumscribe a larger human dilemma whose origins lie in the very phenomenon of language, in the *chaudron fêlé* of *Madame Bovary*'.[80]

VII   Description[81]

Just as the techniques of point of view and 'style indirect libre' are designed to persuade the reader that he is in direct contact with the characters of *Madame Bovary*, so the use of description, both of people and of places, is intended to foster the same illusion. Needless to say, the use of description for this purpose is anything but a novelty, and among Flaubert's predecessors, Balzac is obviously the outstanding example. But, in spite of appearances, description as it figures in *Madame Bovary* is radically different from that to which the *Comédie humaine* had accustomed nineteenth-century readers. For this and other reasons, Flaubert's contemporaries were taken aback by the amount and function of description in *Madame Bovary*. In a sentence which has remained famous, Duranty, in a review of the novel, declared: '*Madame Bovary*, roman par Gustave Flaubert, représente l'obstination de la description', and continued reproachfully: 'En effet, les détails y sont comptés un à un avec la même valeur. Chaque rue, chaque maison, chaque chambre, chaque ruisseau, chaque brin d'herbe est décrit en entier!'[82] Similarly, Barbey d'Aurevilly commented a few months later: 'C'est un *descripteur* de la plus minutieuse subtilité'.[83]

The fact is that those used to the way in which Balzac utilised description were disconcerted by the dissimilarity of Flaubert's technique. In the typical Balzac novel, the author commences by a detailed and exhaustive setting of the scene: the Maison Vauquer in *Le Père Goriot* or Saumur and Grandet's house in *Eugénie Grandet*. This setting will then serve as a constant backdrop to the activities of the characters, which it helps to explain: as he writes of Madame Vauquer: 'toute sa personne explique la pension, comme la pension implique sa personne'.[84] Flaubert does not proceed in the same way at all, with one notable exception, even though he too believes in the influence of milieu. This exception, to which reference has already been made, is of course the description of Yonville at the beginning of Part Two of the novel, and we have already explained why Flaubert deems it expedient to present the evocation of the village in this untypical fashion. Elsewhere, description almost invariably depends on the point of view of of one of the characters. We have already seen how, when Emma first appears in the novel, we are only told about a few details of her appearance as they strike Charles. But while Duranty flagrantly exaggerates the amount of description in *Madame Bovary*, it is true that there are regularly passages, of greater or lesser length, describing this or that location, in such a way that the action is constantly accompanied by, or even replaced by, description. One can understand why, if one looks forward to an important remark he made to the Goncourt brothers when he was working on *Salammbô*: 'L'histoire, l'aventure d'un roman, ça m'est bien égal. J'ai l'idée, quand je fais un roman, de rendre une couleur, un ton [...]. Dans *Madame Bovary*, je n'ai eu que l'idée de rendre un ton gris, cette couleur de moisissure d'existences de cloportes'.[85] He goes on to say that in terms of plot and protagonist his original conception had been nothing like what eventually took shape but that it would nevertheless have been the same novel. It is clear that Flaubert had in mind a certain general atmosphere or coloration some time before the details of the action of the novel were finalised. As Claudine Gothot-Mersch has observed in connection with the original scenario of the work: 'Ce premier scénario prend une allure plus descriptive que narrative'.[86]

It is time now to see by a concrete example how description functions generally in the economy of this work, and for this purpose we can examine a characteristic passage from the First Part of the novel when, a few months after her marriage, Emma is beginning to be bored and dissatisfied:

> Elle allait jusqu'à la hêtrée de Banneville, près du pavillon abandonné qui fait l'angle du mur. Il y a dans le saut-de-loup, parmi les herbes, de longs roseaux à feuilles coupantes.
>
> Elle commençait par regarder tout autour, pour voir si rien n'avait changé depuis la dernière fois qu'elle était venue. Elle retrouvait aux mêmes places les digitales et les ravenelles, les bouquets d'orties entourant les gros cailloux, et les plaques de lichen le long des trois fenêtres, dont les volets toujours clos s'égrenaient de pourriture, sur

leurs barres de fer rouillées. Sa pensée, sans but d'abord, vagabondait au hasard, comme sa levrette, qui faisait des cercles dans la campagne, jappait après les papillons jaunes, ou mordait les coquelicots au bord d'une pièce de blé. Puis ses idées peu à peu se fixaient, et, assise sur le gazon, qu'elle fouillait à petits coups avec le bout de son ombrelle, Emma se répétait:
– Pourquoi, mon Dieu! me suis-je mariée? (pp.45–46).

Perhaps the first thing to notice about this passage is that, while it is largely descriptive, it does not mark a specially critical point in the action. It may be the first time that Emma explicitly formulates to herself her unhappiness with her marriage, but it has been apparent for some pages that she was approaching the recognition that her life was falling short of her dreams. To that extent, and since this particular place is never mentioned again, one may wonder, along with readers like Duranty, why Flaubert bothers to go into such detail about it. Then one realises that the whole scene is depicted from Emma's point of view, explicitly here, since we are told that 'elle commençait par regarder tout autour'. We are put fairly and squarely in her position: this is the first time that Banneville has been mentioned, but we are told about it as though we were already familiar with it, as of course Emma is. That is the inevitable implication of the use of the definite article: 'la hêtrée de Banneville', 'le pavillon abandonné', 'le saut-de-loup'. One then understands that this impression of familiarity shared with Emma dispenses Flaubert from supplying the sort of information Balzac would undoubtedly have been inclined to include. We are not told how far Banneville is from Tostes or in which direction it lies: Emma knows but we do not need to. The next aspect of this passage one notices is the use of the present tense: the house 'fait l'angle du mur', 'Il y a dans le saut-de-loup'. Usually, when Flaubert uses the present tense in a topographical sense, it is a sign that what he is describing has a real existence outside the fictitious diegesis, as with certain details about Rouen: 'le quartier Beau-voisine, qui est plein de pensionnats, d'églises et de grands hôtels abandonnés' (p.241), 'un vitrage bleu, où l'on voit des bateliers qui portent des corbeilles' (pp.245–246), 'Cette espèce de tuyau tronqué, de cage oblongue, de cheminée à jour, qui se hasarde si grotesquement sur la cathédrale' (p.248). In this case, the present tense is a kind of confidence trick, since 'la hêtrée de Banneville' is, so far as is known, entirely invented (in the sketches, Flaubert had indeed called it 'Manneville').

The choice of details is also interesting, some of them appearing meaningful and others gratuitous. Flaubert himself warns us that the dog's circuits in the countryside form a parallel to Emma's wandering thoughts, both representing a circular movement always returning to the same point without having accomplished anything. Similarly, one feels that the state of abandonment of the house, with its eternally closed rotting shutters and their rusty iron bars, figures the dreariness of Emma's life, the monotony of which corresponds to the fact that in this place nothing ever changes. But it would seem arbitrary to ascribe any particular significance to the wild flowers that grow there or to those 'longs roseaux à feuilles coupantes' unless it be a vague sense of menace. They are of course common features of any Norman landscape, and to that extent they are elements of local colour, at the same time as the absence of any apparent reason for singling them out relates to that 'effet de réel' of which Roland Barthes has spoken.

This passage precedes a paragraph in which Emma reflects on her destiny as compared to that which she imagines for the girls who had attended the convent school with her. But it would be wrong to suppose that this means that the evocation of the 'hêtrée de Banneville' functions like the setting for a scene in a play. Had that been Flaubert's intention, the evocation of the place would have been more complete, less fragmentary and more intimately related to Emma's emotions. Rather, what is happening is that Emma's feelings and experiences are inseparably associated with a given physical environment. There is relatively little psychological abstraction in *Madame Bovary*, but there is almost always some indication of the concrete features of the interiors and landscapes which surround the characters at any given moment. However, as in the present case, these indications do not add up to a complete inventory. This is not just a matter of point of view, with Flaubert only recording such features as the character may have noticed, though that is important too. It is also that he wishes to leave a sufficient margin of vagueness in his descriptions for each reader to be able to form his own picture of the place or person. That is why he was implacably opposed to having any of his novels illustrated: 'Jamais, moi vivant, on ne m'illustrera' (Corr., t.III, p.221). At the time of *Salammbô*, he made a crucial declaration, the principle of which is equally valid for *Madame Bovary*: 'C'était bien la peine d'employer tant d'art à laisser tout dans le vague pour qu'un pignouf vienne démolir mon rêve par sa précision inepte' (Corr., t.III, p.226). The significance of this remark is that it constitutes proof positive of the fact that, unlike Balzac, Flaubert has no intention of providing the plethora of information which would make it possible for the reader to visualise a character or a place exactly as he himself visualises it. In that way, it would be legitimate to call his descriptions impressionistic rather than naturalistic.

There is of course one notable exception to this process of selection and fragmentation; that is, as has already been mentioned, the elaborate evocation of Yonville, which does work very much like a stage setting, and we have suggested some reasons (and will come to others) why in this case Flaubert saw fit to depart from his normal practice. More typical of his usual method, even though it is a key event in Emma's life, is the ball at La Vaubyessard. Here we gradually discover the architecture of the manor at the same time as Emma and Charles: first the outward appearance, set in its park, then the vestibule, next the staircase with the ancestral portraits that impress Emma, and finally the salon itself, all that interspersed with the minor events of their entry, the welcome by the marquis, the gentlemen guests they see playing billiards, the reception by the marquise who is briefly described, and so on. So we are told no more than we need to understand Emma's sense of wonder and estrangement at so much hitherto unknown luxury and riches. By such means Flaubert avoids those solid blocks of description which tend to encumber the opening pages of a Balzac novel and crop up at intervals whenever Balzac introduces a new setting or a new major character. Thus we never have the feeling that the narration is being temporarily suspended while the author puts us in possession of information about a place or person. This is all the more true as it is no part of Flaubert's purpose, despite the subtitle 'mœurs de province', to convey information, in the manner of Balzac or Zola, about a given milieu for its own sake. Balzac, Zola and his Naturalist disciples all want to use the novel to tell the reader the facts about some sector of real life. Balzac wants us to know about provincial stagnation in Issoudun in *La Rabouilleuse* because he thinks it should affect our social and political options; the stagnation of life in Yonville is no less grave, but Flaubert has no ulterior motive in telling us about it. The information is there because it is relevant to the structure and intentions of the novel, but not to anything outside its pages.

So description in *Madame Bovary* is not something separate from or incidental to the action. As Geneviève Bollème has astutely pointed out: 'C'est sans doute qu'il n'y a guère de différence essentielle pour Flaubert entre faire une description, faire une analyse psychologique et écrire un roman'.[87] That is another reason why, in spite of appearances, Flaubert is in fact sparing and economical in his descriptions. In his mind's eye, he saw with extraordinary acuity and minuteness the scenes of his novels, but he was very selective in how much of what he saw actually figured in the finished text. In the preliminary sketches, the descriptions are always longer and fuller than in the published version. If one thinks back to the evocation of the 'hêtrée de Banneville' analysed above, one sees that the original draft contains several details eliminated from the definitive text: we are no longer informed that 'C'est un endroit désert, personne ne passe, les arbres sont très hauts', that the wallflowers grow in 'les pierres disjointes du mur', or that there are 'plaques de mousse roussies au soleil'.[88] One may be sure that here as elsewhere Flaubert could see in imagination far more than he thought it reasonable to record. As he was to tell Hippolyte Taine years later: 'Il y a bien des détails que je n'écris pas. Ainsi, pour moi, M. Homais est légèrement marqué de petite vérole' (Corr., t.III, p.562) (in fact, his memory has played him false here, in that, when Homais first appears in the novel, he is described as being 'quelque peu marqué de petite vérole' (p.75): the general point nevertheless remains valid). And when Taine asked him whether what he saw in imagination could be confused with reality, he replied: 'Oui, *toujours*. L'image intérieure est pour moi aussi vraie que la réalité objective des choses' (Corr., t.III, p.562). Flaubert is thus able to describe Yonville with such remarkable vividness that many commentators have been convinced that it must be closely based on a real Norman village, despite all the evidence that it is purely imaginary, even if it inevitably recalls individual features of places that Flaubert knew (it is far from clear why different villages and small towns near Rouen should have competed so heatedly for the dubious honour of having served as the model of a place as dull and dilapidated as Yonville).

It is thus beyond doubt that in all sorts of ways Flaubert's use of description in *Madame Bovary* is profoundly original, which is in part why it so perplexed the readers of 1856 or 1857 who came to it with the sort of expectations aroused by reading Balzac's novels. The best definition of this innovatory quality is that proposed by Geneviève Bollème:

> Alors que jusqu'à lui, la description n'entrait dans le récit que pour le soutenir, le rendre plus véridique, alors que son rôle était seulement épisodique, elle devient pour lui l'expérience unique par laquelle il semble possible d'exprimer les mouvements de la vie. C'est la description qui est le récit parce qu'elle est analyse et expression des sentiments que les choses symbolisent ou supportent, se confondant avec eux et eux avec elles.[89]

But in addition to this extreme novelty of technique, there is another aspect of description in *Madame Bovary* which shocked and disappointed contemporaries, used as they were to description reflecting human emotion or evoking grandiose spectacles of nature as in Chateaubriand, or being applied to sights which were picturesque or curious as in Balzac. A reader as perceptive as Mérimée said of *Madame Bovary*: 'Je trouve qu'il avait du talent qu'il gaspillait sous prétexte de réalisme',[90] a reproach which he expanded when he read *L'Education sentimentale*: 'A chaque scène son petit paysage, très minutieusement étudié et toujours pris parmi ceux qui n'en valent pas la peine'[91] The general complaint was that, in description as in subject-matter generally, Flaubert was, as a supposed 'realist', preoccupied with the sordid and the trivial.

One other aspect of Flaubert's use of description deserves to be considered. That is his scrupulous avoidance of anything resembling the pathetic fallacy. On the contrary, he is at pains to emphasise how independent nature is of human feelings, so that we frequently find nature in its serenity contrasting sharply with the turmoil of human emotions. Here for instance is the scene of Emma's funeral, surrounding the despair and assumed air of bravery of the bereaved husband:

> Une brise fraîche soufflait, les seigles et les colzas verdoyaient, des gouttelettes de rosée tremblaient au bord du chemin, sur les haies d'épines. Toutes sortes de bruits joyeux emplissaient l'horizon: le claquement d'une charrette roulant au loin dans les ornières, le cri d'un coq qui se répétait ou la galopade d'un poulain que l'on voyait s'enfuir sous les pommiers. Le ciel pur était tacheté de nuages roses; des fumignons bleuâtres se rabattaient sur les chaumières couvertes d'iris. Charles, en passant, reconnaissait les cours. Il se souvenait de matins comme celui-ci, où, après avoir visité quelque malade, il en sortait, et retournait vers elle (p.344).

One is reminded of something Flaubert wrote to Louise Colet in 1852: 'Les chefs-d'œuvre [...] ont la mine tranquille comme les productions de la nature, comme les grands animaux et les montagnes' (Corr., t.II, p.119). If a masterpiece like *Madame Bovary* does have that 'mine tranquille' of mountains, it is in no small measure because it contains so much description calmly detached from petty human preoccupations. The same idea recurs in a letter written the following year: 'le plus haut dans l'Art [...] c'est d'agir à la façon de la nature, c'est-à-dire de faire rêver. Aussi les très belles œuvres [...] sont sereines d'aspect et incompréhensibles' (Corr., t.II, p.417). Once again, this reads like an evocation of the impression made by *Madame Bovary*, not least in its scenes of nature.

VIII 'Realism'[92]

From the publication of *Madame Bovary* onward until perhaps twenty or thirty years ago, it was regarded as more or less axiomatic that Flaubert was the epitome of a realist novelist in the sense that he was preoccupied with the seamier side of life which he felt bound to depict without embellishment or idealisation. The reaction in Victorian England was – inevitably – especially violent, and is summed up in a letter written to Flaubert by his childhood friend Gertrude Collier, now Mrs. Tennant and mother-in-law to the explorer H. M. Stanley, who was, apparently with some reason, terrified of her. Certainly her response to Flaubert's gift of his first published novel shows her to have been a formidable and opinionated lady:

> Je ne ferai pas de phrases, mais je vous dirai tout bonnement que je suis émerveillée que vous, avec votre imagination, avec votre admiration pour tout ce qui est beau, que vous ayez écrit, que vous ayez pu prendre plaisir à écrire quelque chose de si *hideux* que ce livre! Je trouve tout cela si mauvais! et le talent que vous y avez mis dans le livre doublement détestable!! – à vous dire vrai, je n'ai pas tout lu mot à mot, car à mesure que je plongeais par ci, par là dans le livre, je me sentais suffoquer comme ce pauvre chien que l'on jette dans 'Il grotto del Cane'.
>
> Je ne comprends pas comment vous ayez pu écrire tout cela! – où il n'y a absolument rien de beau, ni de bon! – et le jour viendra pour sûr où vous verrez que j'ai raison. A quoi bon faire des révélations de tout ce qui est mesquin, et misérable. Personne n'a pu lire ce livre sans se sentir plus *malheureux*, et plus *mauvais*![93]

It says a lot for Flaubert's gift for friendship that, after this thunderous missive, he remained on good terms with the lady. With more moderation in their language, many critics were inclined to share Mrs. Tennant's view of *Madame Bovary*.

As early as the trial, realism was being blamed for the supposedly pernicious quality of *Madame Bovary*. In the peroration of his attack on the novel, Me Pinard specifically incriminates

Flaubert's realism: 'Cette morale stigmatise la littérature réaliste, non pas parce qu'elle peint les passions: la haine, la vengeance, l'amour; le monde ne vit que là-dessus, et l'art doit les peindre; mais quand elle les peint sans frein, sans mesure'.[94] It would be superfluous to multiply the quotations from those who were of the same opinion as Me Pinard or, in more moderate terms, as Mrs. Tennant: it will suffice to mention the entirely typical view expressed by a critic in 1876: 'Avec Balzac, le roman est entré dans ces voies de réalisme brutal qui de chute en chute l'ont conduit à M. Flaubert, et de M. Flaubert à M. Zola – du trottoir au ruisseau, du ruisseau à l'égout'.[95] This filiation was of course encouraged by Zola himself, who insisted that the history of the novel in the nineteenth century consisted in a direct descent from Balzac, via Flaubert, to Naturalism.

Privately, Flaubert was infuriated by these insinuations, and his letters return constantly to this emphatic repudiation of any connection with the Realist school. The main reason for this was his conviction that the Realists aimed at the flat reproduction of reality, whereas his own overriding preoccupation was with the creation of beauty: 'Je recherche par-dessus tout la beauté, dont mes compagnons sont médiocrement en quête' (Corr., t.IV, p.1000). So he regularly and vehemently denies any connection with the doctrine of Realism, even going so far as to aver: 'C'est en haine du réalisme que j'ai entrepris ce roman' (Corr., t.II, p.635). He is adamant that *Madame Bovary* is an experiment never to be repeated, undertaken as a matter of self-discipline:

> Croyez-vous donc que cette ignoble réalité, dont la reproduction vous dégoûte, ne me fasse tout autant qu'à vous sauter le cœur? Si vous me connaissiez davantage, vous sauriez que j'ai la vie ordinaire en exécration. Je m'en suis toujours, personnellement, écarté autant que j'ai pu. Mais esthétiquement j'ai voulu, cette fois et rien que cette fois, la pratiquer à fond. Aussi ai-je pris la chose d'une manière héroïque, j'entends minutieuse, en acceptant tout, en disant tout, en peignant tout (expression ambitieuse) (Corr., t.II, p.643).

Or again, a few months later, to Sainte-Beuve: 'Ce livre a été une affaire d'art et de parti pris. Rien de plus. D'ici à longtemps je n'en referai de pareil' (Corr., t.II, p.710). Despite having to admit the failure of *La Tentation*, he remained convinced that his true bent was for something of that sort, and after having protested about the stupidity of those who believed him interested in 'observations de mœurs', he went on: 'je vais leur triple-ficeler quelque chose de rutilant et de gueulard, où la comparaison [with Balzac] ne sera plus facile' (Corr., t.II, p.727), and that is in part the origin of *Salammbô*.

But while there is no reason to doubt the sincerity of his refusal to accept affiliation to the Realist school, the fact remains that at least in some respects his aims and theirs overlapped. We have already seen that one of his quarrels with Balzac was that the author of the *Comédie humaine* declined to take vulgarity and platitude for what they were and insisted on 'poeticising' them, so that there is some justification for Félicien Marceau's verdict: 'Dans *Madame Bovary*, saluons le premier roman vulgaire de la littérature française. J'entends: le premier sur la vulgarité, le premier où la vulgarité soit à ce point présente, pesante, puissante et agissante'.[96] Flaubert is thus, on the one hand, intent on presenting life as it is, as were the Realists. To this end, he took enormous care to ensure that those parts of the novel which represented or depended on factually verifiable data were as accurate as he could possibly make them. Of course, this is not so say that *Madame Bovary* is in any sense a *roman à clef*: Yonville is an invented village, Emma and Charles are invented characters, whatever their distant origins in the Delamare couple. But there are nevertheless points at which the novel touches on realities which exist outside it, and where that happens Flaubert takes great pains to ensure that what he wrote was in conformity with observable fact. Two episodes clearly required study of medical realities: the club foot operation and Emma's death from arsenic poisoning. The notes Flaubert presumably took in preparation for these episodes have not survived, but we know that he read Duval's *Traité pratique du pied bot*, and it may be supposed that he checked his facts with Louis Bouilhet, who had studied medicine, or with his elder brother, the doctor Achille. He used medical dictionaries for the course and symptoms of poisoning by arsenic. Other chapters in the novel less obviously

77

called for documentation, but still required research. Dealing with Emma's childhood involved him in looking at old 'keepsakes' and children's literature. Given his notorious lack of practicality in financial matters, he found it necessary to seek advice about the operations by which Lheureux inveigled Emma into ruin. For the purpose of the relations between Charles as an 'officier de santé' and Homais as a pharmacist, he had to inform himself about the state of legislation on the practice of medicine under the July Monarchy. For the Comices episode, he took himself off to an agricultural fair. *Madame Bovary*, being situated at an unspecified period during Louis-Philippe's reign, did not require the sort of historical documentation in which he was to immerse himself so conscientiously for *Salammbô* and the second *Éducation sentimentale*, and generally speaking, as Alberto Cento has so brilliantly shown,[97] the documentary basis of Flaubert's fiction increases novel by novel from *Madame Bovary* onward, until *Bouvard et Pécuchet* is almost entirely constructed on documents. Even so, the respect for observable fact is already apparent in *Madame Bovary*, and, despite undeniable resemblances, Flaubert is here departing from the Balzacian precedent. The *Comédie humaine* is packed with a vast amount of information on the most diverse subjects, printing, publishing and the press in *Illusions perdues*, perfumery and the bankruptcy laws in *César Birotteau* and so forth. But Balzac seems to have relied on a prodigious memory and on an extraordinarily varied store of experience for his information – indeed, many of his novels were no doubt conceived to make use of that knowledge and experience. Flaubert on the other hand seems to have been the first novelist who deliberately set out to inform himself on topics of which he had no previous knowledge in order to incorporate that information in the novels as the exigencies of their plot and background required. In that respect, he was an obvious model for Naturalist novelists, especially Zola with his voluminous and painstaking series of 'carnets d'enquête'.[98] In all this, the parallels with the techniques, if not perhaps the aims, of the Realists are unmistakable.

In documentation, as in everything, Flaubert is extremely selective, and he never succumbs to the temptation, as both Balzac and Zola occasionally do, of including more information than is necessary, simply because he has it. If one dissects the club foot episode, one sees that the reader is initiated into the technicalities of the operation gradually, at the same time as Charles, and if one experiences a certain bewilderment in the face of so many rebarbative and unfamiliar terms, that is because Charles does too. But we are only told as much as it is essential for us to be able to follow the diagnosis, the ensuing operation and its disastrous consequences. One can imagine that Balzac in particular might not have been so discreet: one thinks of the long disquisition in *César Birotteau* on the different processes by which bankruptcy can be revoked, when in fact only one of them will be relevant to César's case.

But if Flaubert was reluctant to make a public refutation of those who classified him as a Realist, his friend and disciple Guy de Maupassant was hampered by no such scruples and on more than one occasion stoutly defended his master against such an accusation. The first occasion was during Flaubert's lifetime, in an article signed with the pseudonym Guy de Valmont in the *République des lettres* in 1876. Here the main objection he adduces is that in the general opinion 'realist' was synonymous with 'naturalist' and that people were totally disconcerted by *Madame Bovary* because 'M. Flaubert est un idéaliste mais aussi et surtout un artiste et que son livre était cependant un vrai livre'.[99] On the second occasion, a more substantial essay in the *Revue bleue* in 1884, his argumentation is somewhat different. His first point is that because Flaubert exposes the psychology of his characters by their actions rather than by explanatory dissertations, his aims had mistakenly been conflated with those of the Realists, the more so because of his impassibility. But, according to Maupassant, he was essentially interested in types and remained at heart a Romantic: 'Il suffit de lire avec intelligence *Madame Bovary* pour comprendre que rien n'est plus loin du réalisme'.[100] This contention does of course depend on the somewhat questionable assumption, made by Flaubert and evidently shared by Maupassant, that Realism implies simply the flat representation of reality: 'le procédé de l'écrivain réaliste consiste à raconter simplement des faits arrivés, accomplis par des personnages moyens qu'il a connus et observés'.[101] Clearly by this criterion Flaubert is not a Realist, since he attached such overriding importance to art and beauty.

On the other hand, Flaubert took pride in the fact that in *Madame Bovary* he had produced what he called 'du réel écrit' (Corr., t.II, p.376), and to that extent his aims overlapped with those of his realist contemporaries. Indeed, he arguably went further than they did in the inclusion of the trivial or nauseating details of everyday life: one thinks of the baby being sick on Emma's lace collar, Charles using his penknife to cut the corks of empty bottles, the description of Hippolyte's leg after the bungled operation or the 'flot de liquides noirs' (p.338) which comes from the dead Emma's mouth when her corpse is being prepared for burial. Admittedly, later writers, notably Zola, have accustomed us to even more repellent details, but for all Balzac's supposed audacity, he never goes as far as Flaubert in evoking such disagreeable realities, which is naturally one of the complaints most often made about *Madame Bovary* at the time of its publication, even if it is not explicitly one of the motives for the trial. Flaubert would of course have retorted that style transforms such things from what they would seem in real life. As he declared in 1853:

> Si le livre que j'écris avec tant de mal arrive à bien, j'aurai établi par le fait seul de son exécution ces deux vérités, qui sont pour moi des axiomes, à savoir: d'abord que la poésie est purement subjective, qu'il n'y a pas en littérature de beaux sujets, et qu'Yvetot vaut donc Constantinople; et qu'en conséquence on peut écrire n'importe quoi aussi bien que quoi que ce soit. *L'artiste doit tout élever* (Corr., t.II, p.362).

IX   Style[102]

We have already broached the question of Flaubert's use of language in discussing dialogue and 'style indirect libre' in *Madame Bovary*, a topic we have preferred to treat separately because it is a matter of structure as much as it is of style. But there is much to be said about the originality of his language on a more detailed level. Indeed, Proust, who was not otherwise a great admirer of Flaubert, attributed to his use of language a revolution in our way of experiencing the world no less far-reaching than that accomplished in philosophy by Kant. He defines him as 'un homme qui par l'usage entièrement nouveau et personnel qu'il a fait du passé défini, du participe présent, de certains pronoms et de certaines prépositions, a renouvelé presque autant notre vision des choses que Kant, avec ses catégories, les théories de la connaissance et de la Réalité du monde extérieur'.[103] It may be that there is some overstatement in this, since, by Proust's own account, the essay was written rapidly as a refutation of a piece by Albert Thibaudet in the *Nouvelle Revue française*, in which the critic had argued that Flaubert was not 'un écrivain de race'. But if the polemical context of the statement may have led to some exaggeration, Proust's criticism had the fortunate consequence of inducing Thibaudet to give, in his *Gustave Flaubert* (1935), a particularly elaborate consideration to Flaubert's language, which after more than fifty years remains the best characterisation of Flaubert's style.

Among the characteristics of Flaubert's language which Proust picks out as important in effecting this change in our perceptions the most prominent is his use of the imperfect tense. As we have seen, this use of the imperfect occurs mainly in passages of 'style indirect libre'; as Proust writes, coining the expression 'éternel imparfait' which has become a staple of Flaubert criticism: 'donc, cet éternel imparfait, composé en partie des paroles des personnages que Flaubert rapporte habituellement en style indirect pour qu'elles se confondent avec le reste [...] donc cet imparfait, si nouveau dans la littérature, change entièrement l'aspect des choses et des êtres'.[104] It is of course true that the high proportion of 'style indirect libre' and the large amount of description inevitably entail an unusually frequent use of the imperfect tense. In novels of more conventional narrative, it is normally the past historic which predominates, save in exceptional and experimental cases such as the use of the present tense in Michel Butor's *La Modification*. But it is not just in passages of 'style indirect libre' or description that Flaubert's predilection for the imperfect shows itself. In a very perceptive article, Roger Huss has highlighted what he calls anomalous uses of the imperfect in Flaubert's novels, that is to say, places where the writer employs the imperfect when one would normally expect the past historic.[105] Here for instance is one of the examples he adduces from *Madame Bovary*: it is part of the scene of one of Charles's first meetings with Emma:

> Elle atteignit deux petits verres, emplit l'un jusqu'au bord, versa à peine dans l'autre, et, après avoir trinqué, le porta à sa bouche. Comme il était presque vide, elle se renversait pour boire; et, la tête en arrière, le cou tendu, elle riait de ne rien sentir, tandis que le bout de sa langue, passant entre ses dents fines, léchait à petits coups le fond du verre (p.23).

The first sentence contains a straightforward report of a series of actions, related in the past historic: 'atteignit, emplit, versa, porta'. But while the second sentence continues the same sequence, leaning back, laughing, licking, the actions are converted into imperfects, which totally alters the effect. Undoubtedly, as Roger Huss points out, symbolic implications emerge, and 'avidity and sensuality' are revealed as attributes of Emma. But it is by no means clear that a change of tense was necessary to achieve this result; the choice of gestures would surely have sufficed for that purpose.

In other cases where symbolic implications seem hardly to come into play, the imperfect likewise replaces the past historic. Here is another example cited by Huss, from Emma's panic-stricken despair at the imminence of disaster: 'Tout ce qu'il y avait dans sa tête de réminiscences, d'idées, s'échappait à la fois, d'un seul bond, comme les mille pièces d'un feu d'artifice' (p.319). Here the peculiarity of the imperfect is underlined by the specific notation of the suddenness of a single action: 's'échappait [...] d'un seul bond'. In both these instances, the effect is essentially that of halting the action and converting it into a picture or a state.

Another category of deviant imperfects identified by Huss is what appears to be an iterative imperfect used to relate events of which it is difficult to believe that they happened more than once. For example, this is Emma with Léon at the height of their affair: 'Elle se penchait vers lui et murmurait, comme suffoquée d'enivrement: / Oh! ne bouge pas! ne parle pas! regarde-moi! Il sort de tes yeux quelque chose de si doux, qui me fait tant de bien!' (p.271). It is hardly likely that these precise words were used more than once, as the imperfect implies: no doubt Flaubert wishes to convey the idea that she regularly flattered Léon with remarks of this sort. In this and in some other cases, the use of the imperfect serves to express the feeling of monotony and repetitiveness of Emma's existence and of life in Yonville. The fact remains that the choice of tense represents a curious amalgam of singularity and recurrence.

Roger Huss comments on this unusual frequency of the imperfect that it lends to events a 'pathetic, contemplative, unpurposeful and even static colouring'. A similar impression is noted by Gérard Genette in his seminal essay 'Silences de Flaubert', with reference not only to unusual intrusions of the imperfect but also to other unexpected changes of tense. He points out how often Flaubert records the characters falling silent, then moves to an evocation of some aspect of nature which appears momentarily to have cast a spell over them, and he writes: 'Moments, on le voit, doublement silencieux; parce que les personnages ont cessé de parler pour se mettre à l'écoute du monde et de leur rêve; parce que cette interruption du dialogue et de l'action suspend la parole même du roman et l'absorbe, pour un temps, dans une sorte d'interrogation sans voix'.[106] Indeed, there are visibly occasions when it is not just the characters who turn aside from the action but the narrator himself. Genette picks out one especially telling case when, amid the past definites and imperfects recounting Emma's and Léon's hectic cab-ride round Rouen, we are suddenly confronted with a present tense which cannot relate to what the characters see or notice, since the blinds of the cab are drawn: 'derrière les jardins de l'hôpital, où des vieillards en veste noire se promènent au soleil, le long d'une terrasse verdie par des lierres' (p.250). While in *Madame Bovary* and Flaubert's other novels such present tenses offer a guarantee of the topograpical veracity of some detail detached from diegetic time, there seems to be no cogent reason why this should be important to him here, and Genette is no doubt justified in commenting: 'Ainsi, au point de vue des règles de la narration réaliste, cette description, si brève soit-elle, mais ici encore indéfiniment prolongée par son verbe au présent, est aussi peu "en situation", aussi mal justifiée, dramatiquement et psychologiquement, qu'il est possible'.[107] One almost feels that Flaubert has been momentarily distracted from his story by the recollection of a scene which must have been utterly familiar to him from his childhood. But while one function of such present tenses relating to the topography of Rouen is undoubtedly to remind us that much of the setting of the novel has a very solid basis in factually verifiable reality (or alternatively, as in the case of the evocation of Yonville, to persuade us of the reality of fictitious settings), there are other places where no such explanation appears viable. So it is with the description of Emma at 'la hêtrée de Banneville' already discussed in another chapter, with its reference to 'le pavillon abandonné qui fait l'angle du mur', when the actual setting is of no great significance and where it is hardly necessary for Flaubert to pretend that it is. It is rather as though he has temporarily turned aside from the events of his story to look briefly at some picture which has presented itself to the remarkable acuity of his inner eye. To quote Genette again:

> De *Bovary* à *Bouvard et Pécuchet*, Flaubert n'a cessé d'écrire des romans tout en *refusant*, sans le savoir, les exigences du discours romanesque. C'est ce refus qui nous importe, et la trace involontaire, presque imperceptible, d'ennui, d'indifférence, d'inattention, d'oubli, qu'il laisse sur une œuvre apparemment tendue vers une inutile perfection, et qui

nous reste admirablement imparfaite, et comme absente d'elle-même.[108]

He goes on to note how little Flaubert is concerned with narration as such and quotes a letter to Louise Colet in which the writer expresses impatience with having to produce a passage of narration (the ball at La Vaubyessard): 'Or le récit est une chose qui m'est très fastidieuse' (Corr., t.II, p.83). We have quoted in a different context his disdainful remark about plot and action in his novels: 'L'histoire, l'aventure d'un roman, ça m'est bien égal', and his claim that he only cared about 'une couleur, un ton'.[109] Despite the number of narratives he composed, he was not a born story-teller like Mérimée, Villiers de l'Isle-Adam or Maupassant, and Genette was certainly right to contend that: 'Flaubert est le premier à contester profondément, quoique sourdement, la *fonction narrative*, jusqu'alors essentielle au roman. Secousse presque imperceptible mais décisive'.[110] This is indeed one of the outstanding features of Flaubert's 'modernity', and one of the most significant ways in which *Madame Bovary* inaugurates a new era in novel-writing.

But it is by no means the only aspect of his style which is radically new. Connected with the impression of stasis created by his use of verbal tenses is the effect produced by his unusual technique with the conjunction 'et'. As Proust pointed out: 'la conjonction "et" n'a nullement dans Flaubert l'objet que la grammaire lui assigne. Elle marque une pause dans une mesure rythmique et divise un tableau'.[111] This idea has been eloquently developed by Albert Thibaudet, who remarks on what Flaubert considered a feature of biblical style, the use of 'et' to introduce a sentence, with an effect of solemnity and dignity, as with the presentation of the great doctor Larivière: 'Et il allait ainsi, plein de cette majesté débonnaire que donnent la conscience d'un grand talent, de la fortune, et quarante ans d'une existence laborieuse et irréprochable' (p.327), or the start of Emma's funeral ceremony: 'Et, assis dans une stalle du chœur, l'un près de l'autre, ils virent passer devant eux et repasser continuellement les trois chantres qui psalmodiaient' (p.343), or the account of her wedding: 'Et les chemises sur les poitrines bombaient comme des cuirasses' (p.28).

It is noteworthy that these last two examples, taken from particularly ceremonious episodes, both come at the beginning of a paragraph, which gives them a specially prominent position.

More characteristic still is what Thibaudet calls the 'et de mouvement', which, in a description or a narration, marks a progression to a higher degree of tension, at the same time as it introduces a culminating element, often in one of those ternary phrases which are among the most visible trademarks of Flaubert's style. Thibaudet gives this example; 'les navires à l'ancre se tassaient dans un coin; le fleuve arrondissait sa courbe au pied des collines, et les îles, de forme oblongue, semblaient sur l'eau de grands poissons noirs arrêtés' (p.268). In the same paragraph one finds: 'les arbres des boulevards, sans feuilles, faisaient des broussailles violettes au milieu des maisons, et les toits, tout reluisants de pluie, miroitaient inégalement, selon la hauteur des quartiers' (p.268) (a notation which causes Roger Huss to ask pertinently whether it really rained in Rouen every Thursday).[112] Though Thibaudet's term 'et de mouvement' has been generally accepted, this insertion of the conjunction in fact contributes just as much to the sense of slowing down, since it isolates the last member of a sentence and holds up the transition to the next proposition. An analogous function of holding up the movement is assigned to the unexpected placing of certain adverbs or qualifying terms, often at the end of a sentence. Thus Emma with Rodolphe just before the seduction: 'Elle tâchait de se dégager mollement' (p.165), where, after a somewhat surprising imperfect rather than a past historic, the adverb is displaced to the end instead of following 'tâchait', which is what it logically modifies rather than the infinitive. Likewise, his sentences sometimes continue after the reader expects them to conclude, as in this evocation of the clumps of trees in the garden during the meetings of Emma and Rodolphe: 'ils se dressaient et se penchaient comme d'immenses vagues noires qui se fussent avancées pour les recouvrir' (p.173), where most writers would no doubt have been content to bring the sentence to a close after its first clause.

But if the pace of *Madame Bovary* is slowed by such devices, the forward movement is nonetheless relentless. This is because every carefully wrought sentence has a point to make, and a lot of Flaubert's revisions consist of ruthless pruning: not only do whole episodes, often very painfully elaborated, disappear from the final text – one thinks of the scene of Emma looking at the countryside at La Vaubyessard through different coloured panes of glass, or the hanging of the 'lampions' at the Comices; but words, phrases, details judged superfluous are sacrificed. Thus in the manuscript 'Nastasie sa camisole à demi passée, descendit derrière elle'[113] becomes simply in the printed text: '*Nastasie* descendit les marches en grelottant' (p.13). Explanations are excised if they are deemed unnecessary: describing Charles's embarrassment with his cap at school, Flaubert originally wrote: 'le nouveau tenait sa casquette sur ses deux genoux, ne trouvant nulle part où l'accrocher',[114] then, realising that the point was implicitly made anyway, omitted what came after the comma. The result is that every sentence has a function in the structure as a whole, even if Flaubert is too cunning to allow that function to be too evidently visible. It would be no exaggeration to say that the stylistic tension in *Madame Bovary* is never relaxed; we never have the sense that the language is simply slackening off in anticipation of the next moment of drama or the next decisive event. Again Proust, with an image which has remained famous, has defined the effect this creates: 'il n'est pas possible à quiconque est un jour monté sur ce grand *Trottoir roulant* que sont les pages de Flaubert, au défilement continu, monotone, morne, indéfini, de méconnaître qu'elles sont sans précédent dans la littérature'.[115] Not every commentator appreciates this intensity; Albert Béguin, for example, is vehemently critical: 'Les mots se libèrent de ce qu'ils avaient mission d'évoquer. Plus rien ne compte que leur composition autonome et la place qu'ils ont à occuper dans le déroulement forcené d'un rythme qui n'a d'autre but que lui-même'.[116] Béguin is of course exaggerating, but it is true that the incessant pressure of the style has a lot to do with the impression of inevitability and claustrophobia which hangs over *Madame Bovary*, whereas a radically different technique will be adopted in *L'Education sentimentale*, where Flaubert aims to create the impression of 'le défaut de ligne droite'.[117]

We have just referred to the extent to which Flaubert often refrains from making his intentions in a given sentence too apparent, and, in another context, we have considered the ambiguity and ambivalence of *Madame Bovary* as a whole which so puzzled his contemporaries. This leads to examination of an interesting question raised over twenty years ago by Murray Sachs: 'Comment Flaubert a-t-il su tirer un effet de profonde mélancolie tragique de ces procédés qui sont en large mesure comiques?'[118] The answer to this question is above all stylistic, and resides in the way in which Flaubert combines or juxtaposes two registers normally thought of as incompatible. The juxtaposition can be clearly seen in the deliberate use of something approaching bathos. Having noted that Rodolphe and Léon slept peacefully in the night following the funeral, Flaubert goes on:

> Sur la fosse, entre les sapins, un enfant pleurait agenouillé, et sa poitrine, brisée par les sanglots, haletait dans l'ombre, sous la pression d'un regret immense, plus doux que la lune et plus insondable que la nuit. La grille tout à coup craqua. C'était Lestiboudois; il venait chercher sa bêche qu'il avait oubliée tantôt. Il reconnut Justin escaladant le mur, et sut alors à quoi s'en tenir sur le malfaiteur qui lui dérobait ses pommes de terre (p.347).

The smooth, prolonged rhythms of the first sentence with its two poetic images, give the sense of deep mourning experienced by Justin, but the tone is brutally interrupted by a stark change when the gate creaks as the sexton opens it. Then the emotion is dispersed by Lestiboudois's comic assumption that Justin has been stealing his potatoes. As this paragraph concludes a chapter, the reader is left with both the melancholy sympathy he feels for Justin and the amusement aroused by Lestiboudois's misapprehension. Equally revealing of Flaubert's technique are the places where he seems to be eliciting simultaneous but contradictory responses from the reader. Such a case is the portrait of Emma in the boat bringing her and Léon back to Rouen from their rendezvous on the little island:

Elle se tenait en face, appuyée contre la cloison de la chaloupe, où la lune entrait par un des volets ouverts. Sa robe noire, dont les draperies s'élargissaient en éventail, la rendait plus grande. Elle avait la tête levée, les mains jointes, et les deux yeux vers le ciel. Parfois l'ombre des saules la cachait en entier, puis elle réapparaissait tout à coup, comme une vision, dans la lumière de la lune (p.262).

On the face of it, this is a Romantic picture, with the lovers together in harmony and fulfilment; the mood of elevation is heightened by the moonlight and the sound of the softly rippling water. The sentences are long and regular, with the first three showing that ternary structure so often used by Flaubert to evoke plenitude and satisfaction, and the interpolation of the image 'comme une vision' appears to lift the scene above the level of mundane considerations. In addition, the predominance of liquid 'l' sounds, almost always employed in imitation of Chateaubriand, (no fewer than twenty-six in half-a-dozen lines here), gives a strong sense of poetic exaltation. And yet, if we think about it, we realise that Emma's attitude is purely conventional, we wonder if she is not consciously striking a pose to impress Léon, and we remember that, just previously, Flaubert had mocked the automatism of their tawdrily sentimental responses, when they had thought of the moon as 'l'astre mélancolique et plein de poésie' (p.262), and Emma had started to sing a setting of the archetypal love poem, Lamartine's 'Le Lac', which is subtly devalued when the quotation of the first line is prosaically followed by 'etc.' So is the passage lyrical or ironical? Surely it is both at the same time. Indeed, the whole novel is dominated by the simultaneous existence of two opposing truths: Emma is, from one viewpoint, in many ways a tragic figure; but from another viewpoint, she is in just as many ways a naïve and rather silly young woman (which may itself be part of her tragedy).

There is another way in which linguistically Flaubert brings together normally incompatible features, as is suggested by his already quoted remark to Louise Colet: 'écrire la vie ordinaire comme on écrit l'histoire et l'épopée (sans dénaturer le sujet)' (Corr., t.II, p.287). This means in effect that he has to combine two registers; one epic, the other trivial and vulgar. The epic elements in the style of *Madame Bovary* have been well analysed by Michel Crouzet[119] who picks out a network of allusions throughout the novel: 'c'est la métaphore du combat, de la vigueur militaire, de la robustesse des corps, de la violence indomptée', which connect it to the themes of epic. It is clear too that the use of images in *Madame Bovary* has something of the epic about it. One thinks particularly of the famous image of the fire on the steppes, which is so extended that it certainly ranks as an epic simile, and, though that is a special case, Don Demorest has shown that 'les formes les plus travaillées des images dominent bien plus dans ce roman que dans le reste de l'œuvre de Flaubert'[120] and that 'si l'on a souvent déclaré que les images abondent exceptionnellement dans *Madame Bovary*, c'est à cause de la vigueur du développement (parfois excessif) qu'elles y reçoivent'.[121] This incidentally tends to give the lie to Proust's contention that 'il n'y a peut-être pas dans tout Flaubert une seule belle métaphore',[122] though what he adds to this illuminates the problem Flaubert faced over imagery: 'ses images sont généralement si faibles qu'elles ne s'élèvent guère au-dessus de celles que pourraient trouver ses personnages les plus insignifiants'.[123] It is true, as we saw in examining the question of impersonality that Flaubert does not wish to draw attention to himself as author by inserting images that could not have occurred to his characters (though in *Madame Bovary* he in fact frequently does so). Another feature of epic style is enumeration, which we find in the description of the clothing of the wedding-guests: 'des habits, des redingotes, des vestes, des habits-vestes: – bons habits [...], redingotes à grandes basques [...], vestes de gros drap [...], habits-vestes très courts' (p.28). Even Charles's ridiculous cap can be seen as a parodic recall of epic antecedents such as the arms of Achilles or Aeneas. Hyperbole too is associated with epic, and Claudine Gothot-Mersch presents certain overstatements, notably implausible details in the aftermath of Emma's wedding or the cab-ride round Rouen, as instances of 'exagération épique' (though there may also be another way of looking at them, as we shall see).[124] There is probably too a mischievous intention behind the mention of a line from Virgil in the opening scene. It is of course true that the epic dimension of these features is undercut by the fact that they all relate to very ordinary, everyday things, just as the classical names of Artémise and Hippolyte are bestowed on extremely humble characters.

At the same time, the language of *Madame Bovary* contains many popular or regional elements. Among the terms peculiar to Normandy, one may note 's'ériflait' (p.54), 'embricolées' (p.94), 'ravenelles' (p.46), 'fumignons' (p.344), 'effiloquée' (p.70), 'acres' (p.74), all of which occur in the narrator's discourse, without the italics which elsewhere single out a regional expression not used in standard French, such as 'masure' (p.18) in the sense of 'farmyard'. Popular expressions such as 'braillaient' (p.234), 'bambin' (p.140), 'marmot' (p.95) similarly appear without italics, and certain incorrect turns of phrase, such as 'quoiqu'il lui faudra' (p.124)[125] are taken from colloquial oral usage. Features such as these lead Thibaudet to the conclusion that 'le fond du style de Flaubert, comme de tous les styles vrais, c'est la langue parlée',[126] which is no doubt more true of *Madame Bovary* than of the subsequent novels, and this is one of the elements which enable him to pass, more or less seamlessly, from the narrator's prose to direct speech.

It is of course the contrast between the more oratorical, lyrical style and the freer more 'spoken' style which constitutes perhaps the most difficult stylistic problem which Flaubert had to solve in *Madame Bovary*. The resolution of the difficulty lies partly in the subversion of the more formal, rhetorical passages by means of irony, and partly in not allowing the more informal language to draw too much attention to itself, with the crucial role of 'style indirect libre' as a bridge between the more literary sequences and the direct reporting of spoken French, whether it be in the cliché-ridden pomposity of Homais, the hypocritical blandishments of Rodolphe, the bureaucratic circumlocutions of Lieuvain or the rough speech of old Rouault or la mère Rolet.

There are many other distinctive features of Flaubert's style in *Madame Bovary* which have not been analysed here because, however characteristic they may be and however much they may contribute to the unique colouring of his language, they could hardly be accounted innovations in the history of the novel. They include his detestation of 'qui' and 'que' and the effort he expends on avoiding them, the care he takes in the 'gueuloir' to avoid repetitions of syllables or sounds, his fondness for using verbs with reflexive pronouns where normal usage would not make them reflexive, his pleasure in finding unexpected epithets for certain nouns (Thibaudet singles out 'la hardiesse candide' of Emma's gaze and the 'pesanteur sereine' of Charles),[127] his use of the indefinite article with an abstract noun ('un émerveillement', 'une stupéfaction'). All these things have their place in that highly individual artefact, Flaubert's style, and they all play a part in the sense of solidity and plenitude which it conveys.

That sense of solidity together with the tendency towards stasis and a certain monotony due to the recurrence of certain devices and rhythms (notably the famous 'phrases ternaires') fully justify Jean Prévost's memorable formulation: 'Son style est la plus singulière fontaine pétrifiante de notre littérature'[128] and Jean Rousset's equally penetrating analysis:

> Le plus beau dans son roman, c'est ce qui ne ressemble pas à la littérature romanesque usuelle, ce sont les grands espaces vacants; ce n'est pas l'événement qui se contracte sous la main de Flaubert, mais ce qu'il y a entre les événements, ces étendues stagnantes où tout mouvement s'immobilise.[129]

X   Beauty

In a previous chapter it was pointed out that the main reason why Flaubert refused to subscribe to the aims of the Realists and Naturalists was that, in his view, they were insufficiently concerned with the creation of beauty. It is therefore necessary to consider what he understood by beauty in the novel. Because it is notorious that he suffered from 'les affres du style' and took unprecedented pains over the writing of *Madame Bovary* and the subsequent novels, it can too easily be assumed that for him beauty was essentially a matter of fine writing, as perhaps it had been for a predecessor such as Chateaubriand or a contemporary like Gautier. But in fact Flaubert's theory of beauty in the novel is a much more complex affair.

No doubt its most delicate and crucial aspect is the relationship between beauty and truth. Flaubert once defined his literary activity as 'la recherche incessante du Vrai rendu par le Beau' (Corr., t.II, p.717), and elsewhere he declares: 'j'estime par-dessus tout d'abord le style, et ensuite le Vrai' (Corr., t.II, p.652). Leaving aside for the moment the question of what in this context he may have meant by 'le style', it seems clear that his priority is beauty, even if that is inseparable from the achievement of truth. As for truth, it is apparent that his interest is not primarily in the sort of local truth about the workings of society that is one of the main constituents of the *Comédie humaine* or the *Rougon-Macquart* cycle. Years later, while working on *Hérodias* in 1875, he was to be absolutely explicit about this, but there is no doubt that the principle was well established in his mind long before: 'je regarde comme très secondaire le détail technique, le renseignement local, enfin le côté historique et exact des choses. Je recherche par dessus tout la beauté, dont mes compagnons sont médiocrement en quête' (Corr., t.IV, p.1000). Or again: 'Faire vrai ne me paraît pas être la première condition de l'Art. Viser au beau est le principal' (CHH, t.XV, p.499).

Given that Flaubert knew very well that a novel was bound to reflect the opinions of the author, however discreetly and indirectly, it seems evident how he arrived at his conception of truth. He examined his own impression and experience of life, discarded that which struck him as exceptional, such as his epilepsy or his total devotion to art, and incorporated that core of impression in a character more representative of the common ruck of humanity, in this case the wife of a country doctor who takes two lovers and in the end commits suicide. It is important for him to be able to say: 'Ma pauvre *Bovary*, sans doute, souffre et pleure dans vingt villages de France à la fois, à cette heure même' (Corr., t.II, p.392), when it it would certainly have been impossible for him to make the same sort of claim about Gustave Flaubert. On the other hand, a difficulty arises because, in the normal conception of the novel as a genre, it is necessary to relate a particular story about particular people in particular circumstances. How can the novelist, while avoiding direct interventions and commentaries, demonstrate that what happens in the novel is the result of the general laws of human nature and not of the particular circumstances recounted? How, in other words and in this case, can he show that Emma's fate is ineluctable and not the outcome of bad luck? Could Emma not have found happiness and fulfilment if she had married someone who was less of a nonentity than Charles and taken as lovers someone less spineless than Léon or less heartless than Rodolphe?

Flaubert's solution to this problem is as ingenious as it is original. If we look at Emma's last reflections on her situation just before Lheureux presents his bills, we see that she has reached certain conclusions about her life; thinking of Léon, she finds his image has receded into the far distance, along with other moments of ephemeral elevation:

> 'Je l'aime pourtant' se disait-elle. N'importe! elle n'était pas heureuse, ne l'avait jamais été. D'où venait donc cette insuffisance de la vie, cette pourriture instantanée des choses où elle s'appuyait?... Mais, s'il y avait quelque part un être fort et beau, une nature valeureuse pleine à la fois d'exaltation et de raffinements, un cœur de poète sous une forme d'ange, lyre aux cordes d'airain, sonnant vers le ciel des épithalames

élégiaques, pourquoi, par hasard, ne le trouverait-elle pas? Oh! quelle impossibilité! Rien, d'ailleurs, ne valait la peine d'une recherche; tout mentait! Chaque sourire cachait un bâillement d'ennui, tout plaisir son dégoût, chaque joie une malédiction, et les meilleurs baisers ne vous laissaient sur la lèvre qu'une irréalisable envie d'une volupté plus haute (pp.289–290).

In other words, she wonders, as the reader may, whether what has happened to her has been simply a series of unfortunate accidents and whether, with better luck, things might not have turned out quite differently. But then she concludes that they could not: realisation is inevitably followed by disillusion, 'et les meilleurs baisers ne vous laissaient sur la lèvre qu'une irréalisable envie d'une volupté plus haute'.

It is of course true that these latter considerations are all in 'style indirect libre' and so represent Emma's thoughts, and one has to ask, since in the past Emma's thoughts about herself have been so wide of the mark as to border on absurdity, if there is any reason why we should attribute to this enunciation of a general law any more validity than to her previous misapprehensions. This is where Flaubert's technique is at its subtlest. In the first place, these meditations are interrupted by the convent clock striking four. 'Quatre heures! et il lui semblait qu'elle était là, sur ce banc, depuis l'éternité. Mais un infini de passions peut tenir dans une minute, comme une foule dans un petit espace' (p.290). This last phrase, hardly attributable to Emma's thoughts, thus warns us that her preceding conclusions represent 'un infini de passions'. Secondly, it is immediately after this that Lheureux presents his bills and precipitates her headlong descent to self-destruction. Nothing she thinks after this has any value save as an automatic response to the pressure of events. So, while it is clearly Lheureux's presentation of his bills that is the final straw that brings about her suicide, her meditations outside the convent unmistakably indicate that emotionally she has reached the end of the road. She has recognised the futility of all effort, the inevitability of disillusionment and the tragic limitations of the human condition. In this way, Flaubert has related an individual case-history while almost imperceptibly suggesting that it is illustrative of a universal truth about humanity.

Thus Flaubert combines the story of a single character with a much more widely valid expression of human truth. How then does this relate to the concept of beauty? The first point to appreciate is that beauty is far more than a matter of well-turned phrases: 'Je crois que l'arrondissement de la phrase n'est rien, mais que bien écrire est tout parce que "bien écrire est à la fois bien penser, et bien dire" (Buffon). Le dernier terme est donc dépendant des deux autres, puisqu'il faut sentir fortement afin de penser, et penser pour exprimer' (CHH., t.XV, p.443). Beauty thus involves concordance of theme, structure and language, and each work consequently implies its own particular beauty: 'chaque œuvre à faire a sa poétique en soi, *qu'il faut trouver*' (Corr., t.II, p.519). This means that, in spite of the undeniable presence of recurrent features – ternary sentences, heavy adverbs at the end of phrases, avoidance of 'qui' and 'que' – it would be a grave error to think that Flaubert has a single style reproduced from one novel to the next. On the contrary, he very consciously varies his style according to the subject-matter and the overall conception of the work: 'Il faut que tout sorte du sujet, idées, comparaisons, métaphores' (Corr., t.II, p.110), or, on another occasion, 'un bon sujet de roman est celui qui vient tout d'une pièce, d'un seul jet. C'est une idée mère d'où toutes les autres découlent' (Corr., t.III, p.191). On several occasions, he likewise proclaims: 'Tout se tient' (Corr., t.III, p.164). So, for Flaubert, the beauty of a text resides in the concordance of theme, structure, images and language. There is little resemblance between the tightly-knit structure, the strong images and the sonorous language of *Madame Bovary* and the lacunary movement, the flatness of imagery and the syncopated style of *L'Education sentimentale*, and in the next chapter we shall see with what cunning Flaubert has arranged the architecture of the novel to reflect its major themes.

As for language, we have already noted how Flaubert needed to hold in check his penchant for brilliant images and how he contrives to smuggle them in, despite the restrictions of his code of impersonality. We have also seen how he seeks to produce a seamless passage from dialogue to narrative and to 'style indirect libre'. It is worth remarking in this connection that he had not originally intended to divide *Madame Bovary* into chapters; the chapter divisions only intervene on the copyist's manuscript, probably at the behest of the editors of the *Revue de Paris*.[130] Here too one sees the will to avoid any gaps or breaks which characterises his language, in which each sentence seems to succeed naturally the one which precedes it, and in which paragraphs give an impression of homogeneity. There is no doubt that in *Madame Bovary* Flaubert has attained full stylistic maturity and has now total mastery over his linguistic craft. Compared with the frequently uncontrolled eloquence of *La Tentation*, the sporadic brilliance of *Par les champs et par les grèves*, the language of *Madame Bovary* demonstrates an admirable degree of control. Every sentence has a point and a purpose, which is achieved with great economy of means. And yet there are places where Flaubert makes his effects with a power which verges on exaggeration. One thinks of the extent to which the conversation between Emma and Bournisien is in danger of becoming caricatural, of the fantastic itinerary of the cab-ride. The irony which pervades the whole novel can at times appear over-insistent, as when Flaubert writes, before Emma embarks on her fateful riding-lesson with Rodolphe: 'Charles écrivit à M. Boulanger que sa femme était à sa disposition, et qu'il comptait sur sa complaisance' (p.161), or when Rodolphe closes his last letter to Emma with the seal *Amor nel cor* (p.209).

The big scenes are handled with an impeccably sure sense of drama and an astonishing ability to construct harmonies or disharmonies with varying strands of meaning. No doubt the outstanding example is the Comices, with Rodolphe's insincere flatteries echoed by the meaningless platitudes of Lieuvain's speech, in their turn echoed by the ground bass of the lowing of the cattle. It was not without reason that Flaubert wrote of this scene to Louise Colet in 1853: 'Bouilhet prétend que ce sera la plus belle scène du livre. Ce dont je suis sûr, c'est qu'elle sera neuve et que l'intention en est bonne. Si jamais les effets d'une symphonie ont été portés dans un livre, ce sera là' (Corr., t.II, p.449). But the scene of the Comices is run close by the scene in Rouen Cathedral when Léon's attempts to declare his love for Emma are constantly interrupted by the inane chatter of the *suisse*. Because *Madame Bovary* is such a moving, even tragic story, people sometimes underestimate the comic potential of these and other scenes. But one remembers that, in 1852, Flaubert wrote: 'ce qui me fait le plus envie comme écrivain, c'est le lyrisme dans la blague, le comique qui ne fait pas rire' (Corr., t.II, p.85). In this novel, the emotive and the satirical are often intimately intertwined. A case in point is the description of Emma's feelings after her seduction by Rodolphe:

> Le silence était partout; quelque chose de doux semblait sortir des arbres; elle sentait son cœur dont les battements recommençaient, et le sang circuler dans sa chair comme un fleuve de lait. Alors, elle entendit tout au loin, au delà du bois, sur les autres collines, un cri vague et prolongé, une voix qui se traînait, et elle l'écoutait silencieusement, se mêlant comme une musique aux dernières vibrations de ses nerfs émus. Rodolphe, le cigare aux dents, raccommodait avec son canif une des deux brides cassée (pp.165–166).

This sort of sudden descent from heightened emotion to an incongruously prosaic reality is one of the characteristic movements of *Madame Bovary*. One thinks especially of the two elaborately staged moonlight scenes;[131] the first with Rodolphe, just before he breaks with her, the second with Léon during the course of their idyll in Rouen. In each case, Flaubert uses his considerable powers of pastiche to produce a more than creditable imitation of Chateaubriand: the moonlight, the bliss of the lovers, the gently lapping water, the long, smooth sentences, the elaborate images. But in each case this moment of illusory union is brutally broken. As Rodolphe watches Emma leave, he resolves to put an end to their affair: 'Et d'ailleurs, les embarras, la dépense... Ah! non, non, mille fois non! cela eût été trop bête!' (p.205), and goes back home to write a hypocritical letter sprinkled with water to simulate tears. In the second instance, the boatman is rowing Emma and Léon back from their little island on the Seine, and with very similar means Flaubert creates a mood of union, of happiness and of peace. Then Léon finds a ribbon in the boat, and the boatman explains that it must have been dropped by one of the women in a merry party he had ferried recently: 'Il y en avait un surtout, un grand bel homme à petites moustaches, qui était joliment amusant! et ils disaient comme ça! "Allons, conte-nous quelque chose..., Adolphe..., Dodolphe..., je crois"' (p.263). Emma shivers and the reader divines that Rodolphe is continuing his life of heedless debauchery as if nothing had happened between them.

A somewhat different aspect of grotesqueness is attained when Flaubert, not without difficulty, arranges matters so that the blind beggar arrives in Yonville at the very moment Emma is dying, with the result that her horrific death is accompanied by the beggar's frivolous and bawdy little song. There is, at moments like this, a fairly obvious element of contrivance, but one of the strengths of *Madame Bovary* is that Flaubert does not hold back from such violent assaults on the reader's feelings. This is in stark contrast to the half-tones, to the absence of real conflict, to the subtle insinuations and the deliberately understated style of *L'Education sentimentale* of 1869, and it goes a long way to explaining why *Madame Bovary* always has been, and no doubt always will be, more popular than the later novel.

It can be argued too that in *Madame Bovary* the names of the characters have something of the same vigorous picturesqueness, and Jean Pommier has criticised *L'Education sentimentale* because the names of the characters are less well differentiated than those of *Madame Bovary*.[132] It is certainly the case that in the earlier novel Flaubert has sought to endow his characters with striking names. Originally Emma's surname was to be Lestiboudois, until Flaubert decided to transfer that to the sexton and call his heroine Rouault (perhaps because of the association with wheels and spinning which Margaret Lowe has identified as one of the latent themes of the novel).[133] As for Bovary, it is clear that the syllable 'Bo' or 'Bou' is invariably for Flaubert the mark of a limited personality with a bourgeois outlook: in *Madame Bovary* we also have Boulanger and Bournisien, and in later works there will be Bouvard, Bouvigny (in *Le Candidat*) and Bourais (in *Un cœur simple*). The bovine connotation reappears in the name of the mayor of Yonville, M. Tuvache, and Léon eventually marries a 'mademoiselle Léocadie Leboeuf' (p.368). One or two names seem distantly to echo the functions of the person, notably Lheureux, the successful merchant, and Lieuvain, the 'conseiller de préfecture' with his pompously futile speech. As for Homais, Flaubert himself privately notes the consonance of his name with the Latin 'homo', giving him a representative quality, and as Tony Williams has remarked, the name Binet is appropriate because 'l'activité de Binet est dominée par le binarisme'.[134] Sometimes a name has ironically incongruous associations: we have already mentioned Hippolyte and Artémise, and Emma's supposed piano teacher is Mademoiselle Lempereur. But Flaubert is much too cunning to be over-systematic in selecting names which awaken overtones, and other characters have common surnames such as Lefrançois or Dupuis, or names to which it would be difficult to attach any special significance such as Canivet or Larivière. In this way Flaubert avoids the flatness of nomenclature which displeased Jean Pommier in *L'Education* without falling into the trap of using unlikely names as indicators of the degree of sympathy or disapproval we should have for characters, as Dickens is inclined to do.

XI   Architecture[135]

In the last chapter we saw that, for Flaubert, beauty in the novel consisted, among other things, of a consonance of theme, structure and style. In this connection, it is apparent that *Madame Bovary* is one of the most carefully and cunningly constructed novels ever written, with an architecture which brilliantly reflects its themes. Before Flaubert (and probably since), most novelists have been content to tell a story in linear chronological succession, except where the necessities of exposition required a flashback or, more rarely, an anticipation of future time.

When *L'Education sentimentale* was poorly received by critics and public alike, Flaubert attributed its failure to the fact that 'cela ne fait pas la pyramide' (Corr., t.III, pp.318 and 319), and when Henri Céard expressed his admiration for the novel, the conversation went like this:

> 'Ainsi, vous aimez ça, vous? C'est un livre condamné parce qu'il ne fait pas ça'.
>   Et joignant ses mains longues et élégantes dans leur robustesse, il simula une construction en pyramide.
>   'Le public veut des œuvres qui exaltent ses illusions, tandis que *L'Education sentimentale...*' Il renversa ses grandes mains, fit le geste que tous ses rêves tombaient dans un trou sans espoir.[136]

The implications of *Madame Bovary* are no more hopeful than those of the second *Education*, but there is no doubt that it possesses that pyramidal form prized by its author and which is (quite deliberately) missing from the later novel. Given that Flaubert makes this criticism specifically and solely of *L'Education*, it is no doubt safe to infer that he excepted his earlier novel from it. Certainly it is not hard to discern a firmly pyramidal structure in *Madame Bovary*, and a number of critics have put forward analyses purporting to discover precisely that form.

One of them is Jean-Pierre Duquette, who sees in Emma's suicide 'le sommet de la pyramide vers lequel progresse tout le roman'.[137] But it would be a strangely lopsided pyramid if its summit was so far from the centre. Two possible pyramids have been detected by Pierre-Louis Rey: '*Madame Bovary* [...] fait la pyramide. On peut l'entendre en deux sens; 1) le roman suit une ligne ascendante jusqu'à l'épisode où Emma s'épanouit au sommet de sa beauté, avant de redescendre ensuite; 2) il s'élève constamment jusqu'à ce point culminant que constitue pour finir le suicide d'Emma'.[138] The second of these suggestions is open to the same objection of asymmetricality as Duquette's; as for the first, the blossoming of Emma's beauty is not a pivotal episode, and it occurs after she has already started on a downward path. What may seem a more plausible place for the summit is proposed by Keith Rinehart, who argues that Part II is a smaller pyramid within the larger overall pyramid of the novel: 'The pyramidal structure of Part II reaches its apex in Chapter 8, the middle chapter'.[139] This idea is implicitly supported by Alison Fairlie, when she refers to this same Chapter 8, the chapter of the Comices agricoles, as 'the apex of the book'.[140] This interpretation is more attractive, both because the Comices is such a memorable set-piece and because the chapter presenting it is the middle chapter of the middle section. Even so, several factors militate against its acceptance. Firstly, thanks to Claudine Gothot-Mersch's researches,[141] we now know what was not known at the time of Rinehart's article or Fairlie's book, namely, that the division into chapters was not part of Flaubert's intentions and only intervened on the copyist's manuscript, perhaps under pressure from the management of the *Revue de Paris*. Secondly, the Comices did not figure in the original conception at all, and it was only gradually and at a later stage that Flaubert realised all the potentialities of a scene set in an agricultural fair in Yonville. More significantly, it would be very odd if the structure of the novel hinged on an episode which, however impressive it may be, does not mark a turning-point in the action, but serves only to prepare the real turning-point, which comes in the next chapter when Emma becomes Rodolphe's mistress.

It is therefore reasonable to see if a more logical and convincing pyramid can be discovered in *Madame Bovary*, and there is no doubt that it can. The novel is in fact constructed of two halves, the second of which is a mirror-image of the first. If one sets out from the beginning and from the end of the book, one finds that both necessarily postulate present time. It is unmistakably there in the first person pronoun of: 'Nous étions à l'étude', since, while 'Ils' could be Carthaginians dead for centuries, there has to be someone alive at the time of writing to say 'nous'. Present time is likewise there in: 'Il vient de recevoir la croix d'honneur' (p.356), where Flaubert might have written for example: 'A deux ans de là, il reçut la croix d'honneur', situating the event at some distance in the past. Continuing one's progress from the ends to the centre, one then finds a long passage devoted to Charles alone: Charles on his own before he meets Emma and Charles on his own after her death. Next come two passages dealing with Emma in solitude: the solitude of Emma before her marriage and the moral solitude of Emma in hapless despair once Lheureux has presented his bills. The next stages are the clearly demarcated affairs with Léon: Léon I, as it is customarily called following Flaubert's own notation in the plans, the platonic affair before his departure from Yonville, and Léon II, the consummated affair after the meeting at *Lucie de Lammermoor*. Less often recognised but no less clear-cut are Rodolphe I and Rodolphe II: the first stage of her adultery with Rodolphe, concluded by his satiety with her cloying sentimentality and her realisation of his worthlessness: 'C'est alors qu'Emma se repentit!' (p.178), and her resumption of the affair after the ignominious failure of the club foot operation has put an end to any hope of a reconciliation with Charles which her disillusionment with Rodolphe had made her envisage: 'elle se demanda même donc pourquoi elle exécrait Charles, et s'il n'eût pas été meilleur de le pouvoir aimer' (p.178). In between Rodolphe I and Rodolphe II we find the central episode of the club foot, during the whole of which Rodolphe is mentioned once, only to be summarily dismissed: 'L'idée de Rodolphe, un moment, lui passa par la tête; mais ses yeux se reportèrent sur Charles; elle remarqua même avec surprise qu'il n'avait point les dents vilaines' (p.182). The club foot episode thus marks the pivotal point separating a movement of hope and ascension from a movement of spiralling descent to the final catastrophe, in the course of which Emma retraces in reverse order the stages by which she had risen to what should have been the culmination of her romantic dreams, her becoming Rodolphe's mistress. It is very easy to represent this diagrammatically so as to demonstrate its pyramidal shape:

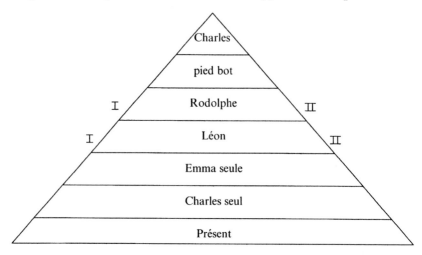

If one then examines the thematic implications of this structure, all sorts of consequences ensue. First of all it can be seen that the dimension of present time envelops the whole novel, with multiple effects. Noteworthy among them is the suggestion that nothing has changed or will ever change. Flaubert even allows himself a solitary allusion to the telling of a story and a temporal prolepsis, in his long evocation, in the present tense, of the village of Yonville: 'Depuis les événements que l'on va raconter, rien, en effet, n'a changé à Yonville' (p.75) and we are warned that if we go to Yonville, in the evening: 's'entrevoit l'ombre du pharmacien accoudé sur son pupitre' (p.74) and that we will still find Lestiboudois cultivating his potatoes in the graveyard, the very graveyard where Emma is now buried. So the stultifying atmosphere of Yonville, symbolised by the triumphant ascent of the odious Homais, the shameless exploiter of the living, and the macabre activity of the gravedigger, the shameless exploiter of the dead, continues for evermore as it always has done. It seems perverse to link the use of the present tense in the last sentence of the book to a particular point in historical time as Pierre-Louis Rey wishes to do. He argues that: 'Une convention implicite veut en effet que dans un roman, le présent narrateur coïncide avec la publication de l'œuvre, en l'occurrence 1856'.[142] Consequently, for him, it is Napoleon III who has given Homais the 'croix d'honneur'. But it would be an exceedingly strange ellipsis if, after retailing the circumstances of Homais's obsequious servility to 'notre bon roi' (p.354) Louis-Philippe, Flaubert were suddenly to leap over the Second Republic and the Coup d'Etat and, with no mention of a change in the pharmacist's political allegiance, were to have him decorated by Napoleon III. In any case, one has to assume that the decoration, like all the other 'événements que l'on va raconter', lies some distance in the past. Like so much of *Madame Bovary*, the chronology here is vague and uncertain, and it is futile to attempt to tie it down to specific dates. For all eternity, Homais has only just received his decoration, which is surely why Flaubert expresses himself as he does in that sentence. The present of the last sentence, like the present of the narrator who writes 'Nous' in the first sentence, is not one which can be related to the realm of real time. The triumph of Homais is not for a given limited period but for all eternity: Homais is always with us.

An analogous effect is attained by having Emma's life wholly enclosed within that of Charles. Charles stands for everything that stifles and ultimately crushes Emma: dullness, prosaicism, stupidity, lack of imagination. And we see her being introduced into this world of his and little by little being suffocated by it. There is no escape. Charles is there from the outset and will still briefly be there after she has gone, even if his contact with her has reduced him to a hollow shell. Not only that; we are not allowed to follow Emma's thoughts until after the wedding. She is already irrevocably shackled to Charles by the time we can share her emotions. We can only approach her through Charles and can only see her through Charles's eyes. Had we been initiated into her feelings and seen Charles through her eyes, we should probably have felt that she should beware of committing herself to him (which is no doubt one reason why we are not allowed to be present at the conversation between Emma and her father after

Charles's proposal of marriage). As it is, when we are finally allowed to identify with her, it is already too late, and the fateful step has been taken. That is no doubt why the novel bears the title *Madame Bovary* rather than *Emma Rouault*.[143] By this device, Flaubert enhances the sense of inevitability, of fatality that hangs over the work. Not only can Emma never escape the mortal embrace of Charles, she never could have done.

In addition, just as at the beginning we are gradually introduced into Emma's universe, so we gradually take leave of her at the end. During her death agony, we cease to follow her thoughts and feelings once she has called for and been rejected by her daughter, and we only regain her point of view briefly, at the very moment of her death, when she has the horrifying vision of the 'face hideuse du misérable' (p.332). Curiously, but certainly not accidentally, the same happens with Charles. At first, we only see him from the outside as though we too were among his classmates, and it is not until he has commenced his medical studies that we adopt his point of view. At the end, we follow his thoughts until he discovers Rodolphe's letter to Emma, after which we forsake his point of view, except for a sentence on his memories and dreams of Emma, and very briefly during his last conversation with Rodolphe. This in itself gives additional prominence to his famous 'grand mot' on 'la faute de la fatalité' (p.355), just as the last return to Emma's point of view does something similar with the vision of the blind beggar. Moreover, this technique of initiating the reader only progressively into the inner world of the two main characters and equally progressively withdrawing from it at the end conveys a sense of the opacity of temperament and destiny, and creates an unmistakable symmetry between opening and conclusion. People have sometimes been surprised by the way in which the novel continues for three chapters after Emma's death, and in his film adaptation Claude Chabrol, despite his desire to remain faithful to the text, felt obliged to omit those final pages.[144] But, apart from the need to to tie up loose ends and inform us of the fate of the secondary characters, by having a certain number of pages after we leave Emma, Flaubert neatly balances the pages we had before we made her acquaintance. In this way, Emma emerges from nothingness and then recedes into it again. Her tragedy has been pointless, in the sense that her life and death have changed nothing, except involuntarily encompassing the annihilation of Charles: 'M. Canivet accourut. Il l'ouvrit et ne trouva rien' (p.356). Emma's death is referred to as 'cette survenue du néant' (p.333). The novel itself grows out of nothingness and returns to it, and one is forcibly reminded of the *suisse*'s apparently stupid but in fact unintentionally pregnant words about the Brézé tomb in Rouen cathedral: 'Il n'est point possible, n'est-ce pas, de voir une plus parfaite représentation du néant?' (p.247).

The pyramidal structure of *Madame Bovary* cannot be doubted, but it is reinforced by other references to pyramidal forms and other ancillary symmetries. Pierre-Louis Rey has commented on the number of pyramid shapes to which Flaubert draws attention in the novel – Charles's cap, the 'pièce montée' at the wedding, the pyramids of exotic plants in the greenhouse at La Vaubyessard, the piles of melons, the pyramids of greengages which Emma prepares when she has guests, even the Yonville *mairie*.[145] If on the level of macrostructure, the second half of *Madame Bovary* is a mirror-image of the first, Flaubert's technique of symmetrical recalls extends also to individual scenes and incidents. One of the most obvious is the inverted parallelism between the ball at La Vaubyessard, which is one of the high points of her life, and the vulgar *bal masqué*, the lowest point of her degradation, which she attends in Rouen just before Lheureux presents his bills. Undoubtedly, the major impression conveyed by this violent contrast is how far Emma has come down in the world, from the supposed glamour of the Marquis d'Andervilliers's château to the sordid realities of the 'restaurant des plus médiocres' (p.297) to which she and her companions resort after their visit to the shoddy dance-hall. But there is more to it than that. Emma may be inordinately impressed by the aristocratic surroundings of La Vaubyessard, but the reader is all too well aware that the duke, who, for her, 'avait vécu à la Cour et couché dans le lit des reines' (p.50), is only a senile old man who dribbles sauce from his slack lips. Her feelings of inferiority at La Vaubyessard are no less illusory than her feelings of superiority in the company of 'un clerc, deux carabins, [...] un commis' and women who 'devaient être, presque toutes, du dernier rang: quelle société pour elle!' (p.297).

Connected with this is the possible sighting of the vicomte, after her last vain visit to Léon to beg money from him. Flaubert avoids showing his narratorial hand by refraining from asserting that it really was the vicomte Emma saw at this desperate moment: 'Mais c'était lui, le Vicomte!' (p.304) – the exclamation mark clearly identifies this as 'style indirect libre' and not a statement of fact. Even so, that Emma should, rightly or wrongly, believe she had seen this prestigious figure from her past, just at the moment when her fate is all but sealed, is yet another measure of how far she has sunk below her romantic dreams.

Another similar recall of her hope and happiness comes when Emma, having humiliated herself by beseeching help from Guillaumin, then Binet, sets off to la mère Rolet, wet-nurse to her daughter and accomplice in her adultery, since Léon could only communicate with Emma by sending his letters via la mère Rolet's cottage. Here Flaubert explicitly reminds us of her most prominent previous visit to la mère Rolet: 'Elle se souvenait... Un jour, avec Léon... Oh! comme c'était loin... Le soleil brillait sur la rivière et les clématites embaumaient...' (p.313). The desire for structural symmetry is all the more apparent as there is no real reason why Emma should go to la mère Rolet at this juncture: the woman is bewildered by Emma's arrival: 'Pourquoi vient-elle ici?' (p.313); there is no way in which she can do anything to help, nor does Emma ask for anything. Admittedly at this point Emma has lost her head and is no longer responsible for her actions, but she might just as well have wandered aimlessly in the countryside. If Flaubert sends her to la mère Rolet's cottage, it is self-evidently to recall a distant hour of harmony and expectation. But it is significant that, whereas on the first visit Flaubert has simply listed the various bits of bric-à-brac that littered the cottage, on the second visit he concentrates on the spinning which Margaret Lowe has picked out as one of the recurrent symbols of fate and enmeshment in *Madame Bovary*:[146] la mère Rolet 's'éloigna, prit son rouet et se mit à filer du lin' (p.313), Emma thinks she can hear

Binet's lathe, and her eye fixes on 'une longue araignée qui marchait au-dessus de sa tête' (p.313). Clearly, this is one of those 'doublets dégradés' for which, as Jeanne Bem has rightly pointed out,[147] Flaubert has such a marked predilection.

Another 'doublet dégradé' is provided by the two appearances of Canivet. When he first appears to repair the damage of the failed club foot operation, he is 'une célébrité. Docteur en médecine, âgé de cinquante ans, jouissant d'une bonne position et sûr de lui-même' (p.186), he harangues Homais mercilessly, carries out the amputation with noisy ruthlessness, and puts the whole of Yonville in awe of him. But when we see him again, in the presence of the great Larivière, who gives him a violent telling-off for the emetic he has administered to Emma, 'ce bon Canivet, si arrogant et si verbeux lors du pied bot, était très modeste aujourd' hui: il souriait sans discontinuer, d'une manière approbative' (p.329). So once again an imposing façade has been torn down to reveal a disappointing reality.

There are also ironic echoes or mirror-images between two of the most carefully worked out scenes in the novel: the Comices agricoles and the visit to Rouen cathedral. Even apart from the fact that both episodes precede and prepare for adultery, there are various similarities beween them. Just as the much-heralded Comices turn out to be a miserable failure (the prefect does not turn up and the firework display refuses to ignite), so what should be the crowning glory of the cathedral, the steeple, instead of being graceful and imposing, is a half-finished and grotesque piece of ironmongery (in the event, it was not completed until twenty years after *Madame Bovary*). Also, in both scenes, declarations of love are heard in counterpoint to completely vapid official utterances: Lieuvain's grandiloquently empty speech and the *suisse*'s parroting of his guided tour of the cathedral.

Two other ceremonious scenes seem designed to set up links in the reader's mind: the two processions, at Emma's weddding and at her funeral. At the first: 'le ménétrier allait en avant avec son violon empanaché de rubans à la coquille' (p.28), and at the second: 'la grande croix d'argent se dressait toujours entre les arbres' (p.344). Again there is the contrast between the hopes raised by the wedding and the bleak finality of the funeral.

We have already discussed in another context the implicit cross-referencing between the two moonlight scenes. A comparable function is fulfilled by a whole network of smaller symmetries and recalls. The most obvious is the recurrent opposition of characters, most notably the eternal rivalry of Homais and Bournisien, always arguing as implacably entrenched opponents, until, after the most violent of their contestations as they keep watch over Emma's corpse, they both fall asleep, 'se rencontrant enfin dans la même faiblesse humaine' (p.339); and, as they awake, the priest pats the pharmacist on the shoulder and says: 'Nous finirons par nous entendre!' (p.341). This symbolic unification reveals that beneath their apparent irreconcilability, they are really at one in their common and complementary belonging to that system of bourgeois values which imprisons and eventually kills Emma.

It would be superfluous to comment on the repeated appearances of the blind beggar and the trouble Flaubert takes to bring him to Yonville so that his little song can be heard as Emma dies horribly. What is perhaps less apparent is the extent to which Homais is made to appear responsible for almost everything that actually happens in the book. It is on Homais's recommendation that Charles decides to move from Tostes to Yonville, it is he who gives Charles the disastrous idea of operating on Hippolyte's club foot, it is he who persuades Charles to take Emma to the performance of *Lucie de Lammermoor* at which she renews acquaintance with Léon, it is he who reveals to Emma the existence of the arsenic, it is he who encourages her to take the piano lessons which serve as pretext for her clandestine meetings with Léon, and if he is not actually responsible for the holding of the Comices at Yonville, it is he who pompously announces their imminence.

One could easily extend these links and contrasts down to the level of microstructure: Emma's tongue licking the last drop of the liqueur when Charles goes to Les Bertaux, and 'la langue tout entière lui sortait de la bouche' (p.332) during her death agony; the white powdered sugar which impresses Emma at La Vaubyessard and the white powder of the arsenic with which she kills herself;

the black butterflies to which are compared the charred fragments of the burning wedding bouquet and the white butterflies to which Flaubert likens the torn pieces of Emma's letter cancelling the rendezvous with Léon; the image of passion as a 'grand oiseau au plumage rose planant dans la splendeur des ciels poétiques' (p.41) and the image of her 'rêves tombant dans la boue comme des hirondelles blessées' (p.189). The connections are almost literally endless.

Of course not all these recalls, echoes and cross-references can be related to the theoretical model of a pyramid. But their number and prominence certainly indicate a strong desire to produce a structure which, far from being unilateral and linear, would be held together by a series of interlocking crossbraces. It is above all this which accounts for what Claudine Gothot-Mersch has so well defined as 'la structure admirablement "bouclée" de *Madame Bovary* [...] Dans *Madame Bovary*, tout se tient, tout est lié: par quelque bout qu'on saisisse le fil, la bobine se dévide tout entière'.[148] The tightly knit structure of *Madame Bovary* is one of the main reasons why it conveys such a sense of inevitability and fatality. For the pyramidal symmetries of the novel are far more than gratuitous aesthetic devices. On the contrary, they are intimately related to its thematic material, to the feelings of claustrophobia, of entrapment which pervade it. The idea of having the structure of *Madame Bovary* so closely mirror its main theme was startlingly original in its time, and, even after almost a century and a half, it is doubtful whether any other novels can compete with it in this respect.

XII   Flaws in the glass?[149]

So far we have spoken of *Madame Bovary* as though Flaubert's object was to create an entirely transparent screen through which we could watch the characters and their actions, as if they were real people and not fictional figures in a novel. Certainly, one of the consequences of effacing the author's presence is to make us forget, at least momentarily, that what we are doing is reading a novel. But it may be that that is not the whole story, and there are signs that in places Flaubert may be playing a game, teasing the reader and obliquely reminding him that all this is just a fictitious construct and that it behoves him to be conscious of the illusion and of the way in which it is built up. There are undoubtedly times when the illusion wears thin and when the screen itself ceases to be wholly transparent. It is therefore necessary to look closely at what are possibly deliberate flaws in the glass in order to discover whether Flaubert has an ulterior motive in putting them there.

In this, one must be extremely careful to distinguish, so far as possible, between the conscious introduction of such flaws and the inadvertent lapses from which even such a fanatically conscientious writer is not altogether exempt. The most glaring example of a lapse of this kind comes much later, in the second *Education sentimentale*, when, as has been conclusively shown, Rosanette is pregnant for something over two years.[150] There is nothing nearly as flagrant as this in *Madame Bovary*, if only because the chronology of the novel is so vague, but there are one or two errors or inconsistencies which are clearly the result of lack of care rather than intention. When Emma's father pays Charles for treating his broken leg, Flaubert writes: 'soixante et quinze francs en pièces de quarante sous' (p.21). This is an obvious impossibility, but we know that he had no head for figures; some notes on the scenarios for *Madame Bovary* show that he had to have recourse to pen and paper for the most elementary calculations, to work out that 3 times 30 makes 90 or that 40 plus 90 equals 130.[151] So the error here is simply bad arithmetic. Similarly, near the beginning of the novel, it is clearly implied, if not specifically stated, that the Rouaults had a son as well as a daughter but that he had died before Emma was born; yet, at Emma's funeral, Rouault says to Charles: 'J'ai vu partir ma femme,... mon fils après... et voilà ma fille, aujourd'hui' (p.346) which means that the son only dies after Emma's mother.[152] The contradiction is insoluble, but again one can see how it arose: penning the last pages of the novel almost five years after writing the opening. Flaubert evidently recollected that he had given Emma a brother but omitted to verify what he had said about him. Slips of this kind are of no literary significance, other than to show that Flaubert was not infallible, especially in matters of chronology and arithmetical calculation.

Much more interesting are those few cases where one may suspect that Flaubert is deliberately stretching the reader's credulity to the point where he will perhaps cease to believe in the factual possibility of what is related and be forced to remember that he is dealing with invention and not with real life. The first of these cases occurs very early in the work: it is the notorious description of Charles's extraordinary cap on his first day at school. We are told that is composed of five elements: 'bonnet à poil', 'chapska', 'chapeau rond', 'casquette de loutre' and 'bonnet de coton' (p.4). As if that were not sufficiently eccentric, we are then informed that its structure, beginning from the bottom, consists of 'trois boudins circulaires', 'des losanges de velours' separated by 'une bande rouge' from 'des losanges [...] de poils de lapin', after which comes 'une façon de sac' surmounted by a 'polygone cartonné' covered by 'une broderie en soutache compliquée', to which is attached, by a long cord, 'un petit croisillon de fils d'or'; finally we discover that it is new and that it has a shiny peak (p.4). It is difficult if not impossible to match up this account of its structure with the preceding statement about its component parts. To make matters worse, we are assured that it is not unique: 'c'était une de ces coiffures d'ordre composite', etc. (p.4), as though we (or at least Flaubert's contemporaries) were perfectly familiar with this species of headgear. It has been argued that this fantastic description was inspired by a drawing in a comic paper in 1833,[153] and in the 1920s an ambitious artist atempted to reconstitute the cap as Flaubert portrayed it;[154] but neither of these hypotheses is convincing. The fact is that, if one tries actually to visualise the cap in accordance with Flaubert's account, one is bound to fail. Of course it is part of Flaubert's intention to display Charles as ridiculous and to present the cap as the correlative of this grotesqueness. But there was no need to invent a piece of headgear so ludicrous as in effect to defy belief, the more so as we are assured, against all verisimilitude, that it is a common type. One has to wonder if Flaubert is not, at the very outset of his novel, warning us that it would be naive to take what he tells us at face value.

The second case of this kind occurs not long after, in the account of Emma's wedding, when we read this: 'toute la nuit, au clair de la lune, par les routes du pays, il y eut des carrioles emportées qui couraient au grand galop, bondissant dans les saignées, sautant par-dessus les mètres de cailloux, s'accrochant aux talus, avec des femmes qui se penchaient en dehors de la portière pour saisir les guides' (p.30). Claudine Gothot-Mersch sees in this an example of epic exaggeration (p.454), and clearly it is hard to accept it as the literal truth. That one or two carriages should be thus carried away by over-excited horses is no doubt entirely plausible, but that it should happen all night an indefinite number of times seems highly unlikely. Once more one asks oneself whether Flaubert is not teasing the reader to see how he can be made to accept something which lies beyond the bounds of what might be possible in reality.

A similar phenomenon occurs with the cab-ride during which Emma becomes Léon's mistress. We are told that the cab goes down the rue Grand-Pont, across the place des Arts, along the quai Napoléon, and the pont Neuf and stops by the statue of Corneille. It sets off again along the Cours and the towpath, by Oyssel, beyond the islands. Then it goes through Quatremares, Sotteville, la Grande-Chaussée and la rue d'Elbeuf, stopping at the Jardin des Plantes, after which it goes through Saint-Sever, the quai des Curandiers and the quai aux Meules, past the hospital gardens, then by the boulevard Bouvreuil and the boulevard Cauchoise, Mont-Riboudet to the hill at Deville. A further fourteen localities, streets or quarters are mentioned, in no particular order. If one tries to follow this itinerary on a plan of Rouen, it rapidly becomes apparent that it is completely unrealistic, and here too Claudine Gothot-Mersch speaks of epic exaggeration (p.461). Again Flaubert is challenging our credulity. Born and educated in Rouen, living nearly all his life close by, he knew the city and its environs like the back of his hand, and he cannot want to persuade us of the literal possibility of such a journey. But one cannot help wondering why he felt impelled to make it quite so incredible.

However, the most noticeable and most disturbing departure from the transparency of the screen is undoubtedly the disappearance of the first-person narrator who relates Charles's first day at school and his gradual replacement by an omniscient and extradiegetic third-person narrator. The shift takes place gradually and without any form of explanation, and so is in no wise comparable to the arrival of the third-person narrator who recounts the last days of the heroes of *Werther* and *Novembre*. Indeed, the last use of the first-person pronoun is particularly paradoxical, since after the account of Charles's arrival at school and of his family antecedents, we read: 'Il serait maintenant impossible à aucun de nous de se rien rappeler de lui' (p.9) – and this before some three or four hundred pages relating the whole of the rest of his life, including thoughts, emotions and incidents of which no classmate of Charles could conceivably have had knowledge. In an earlier chapter, it was suggested that there are important structural and thematic advantages in beginning: 'Nous étions à l'Etude' (p.3) rather than 'Ils étaient à l'Etude', which would have relegated the start of the story to an indefinite past. It is not clear at what stage Flaubert decided to employ a first-person narrator for the opening. The first two general scenarios offer no hint of a first-person introduction. Only in marginal additions on the third (which may be later than the main text) do we find indications that Flaubert is at least considering that mode: 'il était en dehors de nous' and 'peu de notre m intell';[155] this latter phrase, no doubt shorthand for 'il était peu de notre monde intellectuel', finds its way in extended form into the drafts but is excluded from the final text: 'Il n'était pas de notre monde d'ailleurs, il ne lisait pas tous les drames nouveaux, il ne faisait pas de vers! il n'avait pas en tête de maîtresse future! Il ne rêvait pas Paris!'[156] It is noteworthy that, while at no point does the first-person narrator furnish any information about himself as an individual, he does in the drafts several times use the pronoun 'je', but that Flaubert eliminates all such cases from the definitive version. While this anonymity prevents us from taking any interest in the first-person narrator as a character, it is curious that there is already, in the pages for which he is supposedly responsible, a visible shift towards omniscience, when he tells us details about the psychology of Charles's mother: 'Puis l'orgueil s'était révolté. Alors elle s'était tue, avalant sa rage dans un stoïcisme muet, qu'elle garda jusqu'à sa mort' (p.7). How could a schoolfellow of Charles have known so much about the evolution of her inmost feelings? There is thus already a strange anticipation of what will happen when the third-person narrator takes over, so that the frontier between the two is far from clearcut. That must be one reason why first-time readers of *Madame Bovary* are apt not to notice or to forget that there is a transition between two normally incompatible modes of narration.

But even if Flaubert seeks to make the shift unobtrusive, it remains there and remains contradictory. Attempts have been made to explain it away: being used hitherto to autobiographical fiction, Flaubert began in a style familiar to him.[157] Admittedly, there is an autobiographical element in the account of the state of mind of the other *collégiens* from whom Charles was so different. But we know that years later Flaubert read and corrected the first pages of his novel with particular attention to detail; moreover, it is only at the last minute, on the copyist's manuscript, that the author promotes the 'nous' to the prominence of the very first word. So even if the 'nous' might originally have been more or less accidental, it is undeniably something which Flaubert consciously decided to maintain.[158] The conclusion is inescapable; the writer cannot have been unaware that he was presenting the readers of *Madame Bovary* with a blatant inconsistency in its fictional fabric but either thought the advantages outweighed the drawbacks or was quite content to let them notice what Gérard Genette has termed an 'infraction à une norme implicite'.[159]

There is a faint possibility that one other feature of the novel may have as one of its purposes to confuse and disorientate the reader. That lies in its title; we have already drawn attention to the thematic significance of preferring *Madame Bovary* to, for example, *Emma Rouault*. But this choice does have some slightly odd consequences. The first, commented on by the prosecution at the trial,[160] is that, with that title, it is somewhat unexpected to find the first twenty pages or so devoted to a Monsieur Bovary. Then there is the fact that Emma is actually the third Madame Bovary we encounter. The first is of course Charles's mother, and if it is at once apparent that she does not have the stuff of a heroine, we are then faced with a second Madame Bovary in the person of Héloïse Dubuc, Charles's first wife, who may momentarily appear slightly more promising as the central character of a novel, until such time as she suddenly dies. Admittedly it would be an unwary reader who seriously supposed that the title could refer to either of the first two Mesdames Bovary whom he meets. Nevertheless, there may be a faint element of teasing the reader in this procedure.

Until the reaction against Naturalism challenged the pretence that the novel was not a novel but a window on the real world, these peculiarities could only be regarded as inexplicable aberrations. But once writers like Proust and Gide and of course the *nouveaux romanciers* had started using the novel overtly to draw attention to the specificity of fictional illusion, a different interpretation became possible. It might seem fanciful to relate a novel apparently conventional in its form and intentions to some of the more extreme experiments of the *nouveau roman*, were there not irrefutable documentary evidence that Flaubert came very close to forcing the reader to take cognisance of the conditions of the illusory experience he was undergoing. The evidence lies in his plans for an epilogue to the novel, to be placed after the award of Homais's decoration. The first sign comes on what is known as Scenario LXX in the Pommier-Leleu edition (p.60 of the Leclerc facsimile edition), where after the words 'Il vient de recevoir la croix d'honneur', one reads 'Epilogue', with no further explanation. But the next scenario is much fuller and more revealing. Here is the original sketch, before the various interlinear and marginal modifications which the writer later made to it:

> Le jour qu'il l'a reçu n'y voulut pas croire. Mr X député lui avait envoyé un bout de ruban – le met se regarde dans la glace éblouissement. –
>
> il participait à ce rayon de gloire qui commençant au Sous-préfet qui était chevalier allait par le préfet qui était officier le génér de division qui était commandeur – les min gds-off, jusqu'au monarque qui était gd-croix que dis-je jusqu'à l'Emp Napol qui l'a créé – Homais s'absorbait dans le soleil d'Austerlitz
>
> tous les aspects de la croix. institut – diplomate – guerrier – à en crever
>
> et c'est un des plus gdes preuves de son temperament qu'il n'en soit pas crevé.[161]

Up to this point, it looks as though Flaubert's aim is simply to exaggerate Homais's conceit and excitement to the point of an absurd delirium, and that is how most commentators have read it. But in the second part of the sketch, the aim becomes much more radical:

> Doute de lui – regarde les bocaux – doute de son existence – ne suis-je qu'un personnage de roman, le fruit d'une imagination en délire, l'invention d'un petit paltaquot[162] que j'ai vu naître – Oh cela n'est possible. Voilà les fœtus.
>
> Puis se résumant par le gd mot du rationalisme moderne Cogito; ergo sum.

Self-evidently, this epilogue would have totally exploded the idea that *Madame Bovary* was anything other than a fictional construct. Homais asking if he is not a fictitious character created by a certain Gustave Flaubert can only receive the answer: 'Yes, you are'. And of course if Homais is only a character in a novel, then so are all the others, and *Madame Bovary* becomes a self-referential work.

But, startling as this idea is, Flaubert does not stop there. Two additions seem intended simply to intensify Homais's delirium. The first comes after 'doute de son existence': 'délire. effets fantastiques. Sa croix répétée dans les glaces, pluie foudre de ruban'. The other follows 'les fœtus' and adds to the things Homais looks at for reassurance: 'voilà mes enfants voilà voilà'.

But the third, much more far-reaching, is inserted after the reference to the 'petit paltaquot que j'ai vu naître' and reads: '& qui m'a inventé pr faire croire que je n'existe pas'. After having virtually admitted that he exists only in a novelist's imagination, Homais now claims that the novelist invented him to make people believe he did not really exist. So Flaubert postulates a fictitious Homais masking a real Homais, giving rise to a fictitious Homais and so *ad infinitum*. The reader would have been completely lost and demoralised, and the novel would have dissolved before his eyes. To make matters worse, on a partial scenario drafted shortly before the projected epilogue, Flaubert has noted an equation which has remained famous: 'Homais vient de Homo = l'homme'.[163] To try to reassure himself, Homais has recourse to the Cartesian maxim: 'I think, therefore I am'. But in Homais's case, we know this not to be true; he *is* not. In that case, and if, as the equation implies, Homais is the representative of humanity, can we be sure that we really exist and are not figments of some cosmic imagination? The epilogue would have turned *Madame Bovary* into one of the most insidiously subversive novels ever written.

It can naturally be objected that the idea of this epilogue was only a passing fancy, possibly conceived at an early stage in the genesis of the novel, as some commentators have suggested, and that it would be rash to interpret it as relevant to Flaubert's eventual intentions. But in fact it is possible to assign an approximate date to the two scenarios mentioning the epilogue, and it has been shown that both were written no earlier than June or July 1855 and perhaps a month or two later.[164] The significance of this late date is not to be missed. Virtually nine-tenths of the final text were complete when Flaubert had the totally unexpected notion of introducing a vastly different viewpoint into it, and bringing firmly to the notice of us readers that we were reading a work of fiction by a young whippersnapper named Gustave Flaubert. It is of course true that the idea was evidently not taken any further; on the other hand, the sketch of the epilogue contains verbs in the past tense and proper sentences, which indicates that the author had thought it through carefully and gone beyond the stage of brief notes for a vague possibility. That, only a few months before sending off the copyist's manuscript to Maxime Du Camp for his *Revue de Paris*, Flaubert should have contemplated destroying the illusion that the reader was looking at a directly observed and recorded reality is strong evidence that in his mind *Madame Bovary* was potentially an even more radical innovation in novel-writing than its apparently conventional form might suggest.

If then one looks at what might be flaws in the glass in the light of the proven hesitation, demonstrated by the projected epilogue, over the maintenance or destruction of the illusion of reality, it begins to appear likely that Flaubert was on the verge of making *Madame Bovary* into a much more 'modern' novel than at first appears. On the basis of an unrealised and abandoned epilogue, it would be a great exaggeration to see the novel as a clear precursor of the *nouveau roman*. The idea of a novel questioning the established conventions of the genre to which it nominally belongs is not new: one thinks of *Tristram Shandy*, of *Jacques le Fataliste et son maître*, and, nearer to Flaubert's own time, Nodier's *Histoire du roi de Bohême et de ses sept châteaux*. It is nevertheless surprising to realise that a novel which for so long passed as the model of realism has features which foreshadow some of the aspects of the experimental novels of the twentieth century. Perhaps it is this side of *Madame Bovary* which accounts for the favour it continues to enjoy among present-day practitioners of the novel.

XIII   Conclusion

A number of features of the greatness and perennial popularity of *Madame Bovary* have not figured in the foregoing analyses because they represent the continuation of a tradition rather than a departure from it. The anatomisation of a certain feminine psychology is noteworthy among them. But there has always been a predilection in the French novel for detailed investigation of the problems and emotions of women – from *La Princesse de Clèves* through the *Vie de Marianne, Manon Lescaut* in the eighteenth century to *Corinne, Carmen, Colomba* and numerous novels by Balzac in Flaubert's own time. Similarly, the satirical depiction of middle-class *mores* has been a favourite theme in works such as *Le Roman bourgeois, Gil Blas* and *Le Paysan parvenu* through to Balzac's *César Birotteau* and Champfleury's *Les Bourgeois de Molinchart*. There is also a certain fascination in the characterisation of small-town life in provincial France, as we find in various Balzac novels – Saumur in *Eugénie Grandet*, Issoudun in *La Rabouilleuse*, Guérande in *Béatrix* and so on. But whatever the importance of these elements in the overall stature of *Madame Bovary*, one could hardly maintain that they are innovations in the history of the novel.

On the other hand, there is one aspect of *Madame Bovary* that is so all-pervasive that it was not possible to devote a special chapter to it. That is the question of irony. Irony is present in *Madame Bovary* from the first page to the last, on multiple levels and often where it is least expected. Irony naturally dominates the satirical side of the work, in the portraits of Homais, Bournisien, Binet, Charles, Lheureux and others: in this, *Madame Bovary* is no doubt not radically different from *Gil Blas*, certain novels by Balzac or even Pigault-Lebrun. What is less expected is the constant irony about Emma herself. Referring to the conversation between Emma and Léon on the evening of the Bovarys' arrival in Yonville, Flaubert writes: 'Ce sera, je crois, la première fois que l'on verra un livre qui se moque de sa jeune première et de son jeune premier' (Corr., t.II, p.172). In fact, the irony here is, as so often, double-edged. Certainly, there is mockery of the inanities exchanged by the two interlocutors, notably in the anecdote of the great pianist who had his instrument transported to some Alpine beauty-spot so as to play with more inspiration. On the other hand, if Emma may for the time being plausibly be regarded as the 'jeune première', there is already some evidence that Léon is hardly cut out to be the 'jeune premier', and of course he subsequently falls far short of that status. The fact is that in *Madame Bovary* there is in reality neither a hero nor a heroine, an aspect of the novel that displeased Sainte-Beuve and was partly responsible for the charge of immorality.

Emma herself is bathed in an ambivalently ironic light. If, as Flaubert maintains, 'une âme se mesure à la dimension de son désir' (Corr., t.II, p.329), she is, with her immaterial longings, by far superior to the narrow-minded creatures who surround her – Charles, happy with a monotonous job, a pretty wife, and a well-kept household, Rodolphe, with the satisfaction of his sensual desires and cheap pleasures, Homais with his implacable conceit and self-aggrandisement, Lheureux with his financial machinations and so forth. To that extent, there is something incontestably tragic about her downfall. But at the same time, with her head full of pictures and notions culled from third-rate novelettes, she is too naïve to see through Rodolphe's callous philandering or Léon's pusillanimity, and her actions and reactions are often stereotyped and unintelligent. She is taken in not only by those who seek to deceive and outwit her, such as Rodolphe and Lheureux, but also by those like Charles of whom she can see only a few of his outward characteristics.

There is constant irony too in the juxtaposition of contrasting scenes, as in the divergent reactions of Emma and Charles after the humiliating failure of the club-foot operation or the anticlimaxes after the two moonlight scenes. Lyrical and emotive passages are regularly undercut by allusions to a particularly prosaic reality. There is dramatic irony when Charles politely informs Rodolphe that Emma is at his disposal and when Bournisien implicitly likens Emma's melancholy to 'une vache qui avait l'*enfle*'.

There is latent irony in misplaced classical allusions and inapposite names. There is irony every time Homais opens his mouth or picks up his pen and launches into one of his pretentious tirades. There is bitter irony in having the novel conclude, not with the death of Emma or that of Charles, but with the ultimate triumph of Homais and all he stands for.

One can even argue that there is irony in persuading us for three or four hundred pages that we are looking at a real 'slice of life' and at the last minute only just holding back from telling us that we have been duped by a novelist telling us a pack of lies. Admittedly, Flaubert refrained from this ultimate act of destruction, but there are nevertheless signs that he is not averse to playing ironic games with his readers. 'L'ironie pourtant me semble dominer la vie' he once commented (Corr., t.II, p.84). Irony in the novel is of course anything but a new phenomenon, and several of Flaubert's favourite novelists were expert practitioners of the art – Rabelais, Voltaire, Fielding among others. What seems to distinguish his manipulation of irony from that of his predecessors is the extent to which it is multidirectional. Most often, of course, the target of the irony is the petty-mindedness of the bourgeoisie of Yonville. But sometimes Flaubert seems to want to aim it at the unwary reader. We have seen how, in the two moonlight scenes, he creates a mood of elevation and plenitude, only to destroy it brutally, as though he were taking pleasure in misleading the reader into taking seriously something which will prove to be fake.

Irony is thus everywhere detectable in the novel, which thereby becomes profoundly ambivalent. One could even maintain that the one topic which in Flaubert's thought and letters, namely Art, which appears exempt from ironic devaluation, is in *Madame Bovary* subtly and indirectly undermined. This is done through the person of Binet, who is in many ways the caricature of the artist, as Flaubert hints when we first meet him, telling us that 'il s'amusait à tourner des ronds de serviette dont il encombrait sa maison, avec la jalousie d'un artiste et l'égoïsme d'un bourgeois' (p.77). In one of his letters, Flaubert once said that his own future consisted of 'une main de papier blanc qu'il faut couvrir de noir, uniquement pour ne pas crever d'ennui et "comme on a un tour sans son grenier quand on habite la campagne!'" (Corr., t.IV, p.526), and the comparison occurs from time to time, as when he writes: 'Je continue à tourner mes ronds de serviette' (Corr., t.IV, p.646). This constant irony is certainly one of the main features of the modernity of *Madame Bovary* and one of the sources of its enduring fascination for commentators and ordinary readers alike, but it is also one of the reasons why it is so difficult to adapt it for stage, cinema or television, where it is so much harder to render the hidden implications of a word or a sentence which, while apparently saying one thing, is simultaneously suggesting another.

But if the omnipresence of irony brings *Madame Bovary* close to many of the great novels of the twentieth century, all sorts of other elements likewise seem to detach it from most of its contemporaries. The comparison with Balzac is especially enlightening. As we have seen, Flaubert's attitude to the author of the *Comédie humaine* is compounded of almost equal proportions of admiration and irritation – admiration for the immensity of his achievement, irritation with his constant expression of his own opinions and prejudices, and with his cavalier treatment of the French language. So, while the advice of Bouilhet and Du Camp guided him towards a type of novel related to that which Balzac had cultivated, he was firmly convinced that what he had it in mind to produce in *Madame Bovary* would be quite unlike the Balzacian model – in its style, in its construction, in its refusal to glamourise or exaggerate, in its forswearing of authorial interventions. This intention led to many new techniques of narration, through the use of point of view, through the prominence of *style indirect libre*, through the dominance of description over straight narration.

By no means all of these innovations were appreciated, let alone assimilated, in Flaubert's own time, but their number and significance mean that *Madame Bovary* stands on the very cusp of modernity, and that the history of the novel after 1857 would have been very different had Bouilhet and Du Camp not forced their friend to rethink the direction of his fiction. As Sartre wrote in 1966, 'Flaubert, créateur du roman "moderne", est au centre de toutes nos préoccupations littéraires actuelles',[165] a verdict confirmed a few years later by Bernard Masson: 'Flaubert est au centre de toute réflexion moderne sur le métier d'écrire et la finalité de l'œuvre littéraire'.[166] It is of course impossible to distinguish how much this position owes to Flaubert in general and how much to *Madame Bovary* in particular, and there is no doubt that Flaubert further widened the frontiers of the novel with *L'Education sentimentale* and *Bouvard et Pécuchet*, if perhaps not with *Salammbô*, to say nothing of the immense impact of his correspondence. But it is certain that *Madame Bovary* is one of the most profoundly original novels ever written and that it radically affected the course of subsequent literature.

Bibliography

The bibliography concerning *Madame Bovary* and Flaubert in general is so immense that I have had to restrict myself to listing books and articles specifically mentioned in what precedes. Anyone requiring more information should turn to the four excellent volumes of D. J. Colwell's *Bibliographie des Etudes sur Gustave Flaubert (1857–1988)* Egham, Runnymede Books, 1989–1990.

EDITIONS OF WORKS BY FLAUBERT

Œuvres complètes, Paris, Club de l'Honnête Homme, 1971–1976.

Correspondance, ed. Jean Bruneau, Paris, Bibliothèque de la Pléiade, 1973–1997.

Madame Bovary, ed. René Dumesnil, Paris, Les Belles Lettres, 1945.

Madame Bovary, ed. Paul Vernière, Paris, Editions de Cluny, 1951.

Madame Bovary, with an introduction by Félicien Marceau, Paris, Livre de Poche, 1961.

Madame Bovary, ed. Claudine Gothot-Mersch, Paris, Garnier, 1971.

Madame Bovary, ed. Jacques Neefs, Paris, Livre de Poche classique, 1999.

Madame Bovary. *Nouvelle Version précédée des scénarios inédits*, ed. Jean Pommier and Gabrielle Leleu, Paris, Corti, 1949.

Plans et Scénarios de Madame Bovary, ed. Yvan Leclerc, Paris, Editions du CNRS, Zulma, 1995.

Souvenirs, Notes et Pensées intimes, ed. J.P. Germain, Paris, Nizet, 1987.

Par les champs et par les grèves, ed. Adrianne Tooke, Geneva, Droz, 1987.

Pour Louis Bouilhet, ed. Alan Raitt, Exeter University Press, 1994.

BOOKS AND ARTICLES DEALING WHOLLY OR PARTLY WITH FLAUBERT AND/OR *MADAME BOVARY*

AHLSTRÖM, Anna: *Etude sur la langue de Flaubert*, Macon, Privat, 1899.

BARNES, Julian: 'Justin: A Small Major Character', in *The Process of Art. Studies in Nineteenth-Century French Literature and Art offered to Alan Raitt*, ed. M.J. Freeman *et al.*, Oxford, Clarendon Press, 1998.

BARNES, Julian: 'Letter from Genoa', *Times Literary Supplement*, November 26, 1999.

BART, B.F.: *Flaubert's Landscape Descriptions*, Ann Arbor, University of Michigan Press, 1956.

BEM, Jeanne: *Clefs pour* L'Education sentimentale, Tübingen, Narr / Paris, Place, 1981.

BINSWANGER, Paul:. *Die ästhetische Problematik Flauberts. Untersuchungen zum Problem von Sprache und Stil in der Literatur*, Frankfurt, Klostermann, 1934.

BISMUT, Roger: 'Flaubert et *Le Médecin de campagne* de Balzac', *Les Amis de Flaubert*, mai 1965.

BISMUT, Roger: 'Sur une Chronologie de *Madame Bovary*', *Les Amis de Flaubert*, mai 1973.

BOLLEME, Geneviève: *La Leçon de Flaubert*, Paris, Julliard, 1964.

BONWIT, Marianne: *Gustave Flaubert et le principe d'impassibilité*, Berkeley and Los Angeles, University of California Publications in Modern Philology, Vol.33, no.4, 1950.

BOPP, Leon: *Commentaire sur* Madame Bovary, Neuchâtel, La Baconnière, 1951.

BROMBERT, Victor: 'La première *Education sentimentale*. Roman de l'artiste', *Europe*, septembre–octobre–novembre, 1969.

BRUNEAU, Jean: *Les Débuts littéraires de Gustave Flaubert 1831–1845*, Paris, Colin, 1962.

BRUNEAU, Jean: *Le* Conte oriental *de Gustave Flaubert*, Paris, Denoel, 1973.

BRUNEAU, Jean: 'La Famille Collier et Flaubert', *Nineteenth-Century French Studies*, Fall–Winter, 1988–1989.

BUCK, Stratton: 'The Chronology of the *Education sentimentale*', *Modern Language Notes*, February, 1952.

CENTO, Alberto: *Il Realismo documentario nell'*Education sentimentale, Naples, Liguori, 1967.

CROUZET, Michel: 'Le Style épique dans *Madame Bovary*', *Europe*, septembre–octobre–novembre, 1969.

CULLER, Jonathan: *Flaubert: The Uses of Uncertainty*, London, Elek, 1974.

DEMOREST, Don: *L'Expression figurée et symbolique dans l'œuvre de Gustave Flaubert*, Geneva, Slatkine Reprints, 1967.

DESCHARMES, René: *Flaubert; sa vie, son caractère, ses idées avant 1857*, Paris, Ferroud, 1909.

DESCHARMES, René and René Dumesnil: *Autour de Flaubert*, Paris, Mercure de France, 1912.

DIVERSE: *Autour d'Emma Bovary. Un film de Claude Chabrol avec Isabelle Huppert*, Paris, Hatier, 1991.

DU CAMP, Maxime: *Souvenirs littéraires*, 3e édition, Paris, Hachette, 1906.

DUCHET, Claude: 'Discours social et texte italique dans *Madame Bovary*', *Langages de Flaubert*, ed. M. Issacharoff, Paris, Lettres Modernes, 1976.

DUMESNIL, René: *La Vocation de Flaubert*, Paris, Gallimard, 1961.

DUQUETTE, Jean-Pierre: *Flaubert ou l'Architecture du Vide*, Presses de l'Université de Montréal, 1972.

DURRY, Marie-Jeanne: *Flaubert et ses Projets inédits*, Paris, Nizet, 1950.

FAIRLIE, Alison: *Flaubert:* Madame Bovary, London, Arnold, 1962.

FALCONER, Graham: 'Flaubert Assassin de Charles', *Langages de Flaubert*, ed. M. Issacharoff, Paris, Lettres Modernes, 1976.

FERRERE, E.-L.: *L'Esthétique de Gustave Flaubert*, Paris, Conard, 1913.

GANS, E.L.: *The Discovery of Illusion. Flaubert's Early Works 1835–1837*, Berkeley, University of California Press, 1971.

GENETTE, Gérard: *Figures*, Paris, Seuil, 1966.

GENETTE, Gérard: *Figures III*, Paris, Seuil, 1972.

GLEIZE, Joelle: 'Le Défaut de ligne droite', *Littérature*, octobre 1974.

GONCOURT, Edmond et Jules de: *Journal*, ed. Robert Ricatte, Paris, Fasquelle–Flammarion, 1956.

GOTHOT-MERSCH, Claudine: *La Genèse de* Madame Bovary, Paris, Corti, 1966.

GOTHOT-MERSCH, Claudine: 'Le Point de vue dans *Madame Bovary*', *Cahiers de l'Association Internationale des Etudes Françaises*, 1971.

GOTHOT-MERSCH, Claudine: 'De *Madame Bovary* à *Bouvard et Pécuchet*. La Parole des personnages dans les romans de Flaubert', *Revue d'Histoire littéraire de la France*, juillet–octobre 1981.

HAIG, Stirling: *Flaubert and the Gift of Speech. Dialogue and Discourse in Four 'Modern' Novels*, Cambridge University Press, 1986.

HEATH, Stephen: *Flaubert:* Madame Bovary, Cambridge University Press, 1992.

HUSS, Roger: 'Some anomalous Uses of the Imperfect and the Status of Action in Flaubert', *French Studies*, XXXI, 1977.

JAMES, Henry: 'Gustave Flaubert', in *Selected Criticism*, ed. M. Shapira, London, Heinemann, 1968.

LOWE, Margaret: *Towards the Real Flaubert. A Study of* Madame Bovary, Oxford, Clarendon Press, 1984.

MASON, Germaine: 'Les Deux Clairs de lune de *Madame Bovary*', *French Studies*, July 1954.

MASON, Germaine: *Les Ecrits de jeunesse de Flaubert*, Paris, Nizet, 1961.

MASSON, Bernard: presentation of *Gustave Flaubert I: Flaubert et après*, Paris, Lettres Modernes, 1984.

MATHET, Marie-Thérèse: *Le Dialogue romanesque chez Flaubert*, Paris, Aux Amateurs de Livres, 1988.

MAUPASSANT, Guy de: *Pour Gustave Flaubert*, Bruxelles, Complexe, 1986.

MAYNIAL, Edouard: *La Jeunesse de Flaubert*, Paris, Mercure de France, 1913.

MEIN, Margaret: 'Flaubert, a Precursor of Proust', *French Studies*, XVII, 1963.

MOUCHARD, Claude and Jacques Neefs: *Flaubert*, Paris, Balland, 1986.

NAAMAN, Antoine Youssef: *Les Débuts de Gustave Flaubert et sa technique de la description*, Paris, Nizet, 1962.

NATUREL, Mireille: *Flaubert et Proust; un secret d'écriture*, Amsterdam / Atlanta, Rodopi, 1999.

PINATEL, Joseph: 'Notes vétilleuses sur la chronologie de *L'Education sentimentale*', *Revue d'Histoire littéraire de la France*, janvier–mars 1953.

PISTORIUS, George: 'La Structure des comparaisons dans *Madame Bovary*', *Cahiers de l'Association Internationale des Etudes Françaises*, 1971.

POMMIER, Jean: '*La Muse du Département* et le thème de la femme mal mariée chez Balzac, Mérimée et Flaubert', *L'Année balzacienne*, 1961.

POMMIER, Jean: 'Noms et Prénoms dans *Madame Bovary*: essai d'onomastique littéraire' in *Dialogues avec le passé*, Paris, Nizet, 1976.

PREVOST, Jean: quoted by Jean-Pierre Richard, *Littérature et Sensation. Stendhal, Flaubert*, Paris, Seuil, 1970, p.237.

PROUST, Marcel: *Sur Baudelaire, Flaubert et Morand*, Bruxelles, Complexe, 1987.

RAITT, Alan: 'Nous étions à l'étude...', *Gustave Flaubert II*, Paris, Lettres Modernes, 1986.

RAITT, Alan: 'Le Balzac de Flaubert', *L'Année balzacienne*, 1991.

RAITT, Alan: 'The Date of the Projected Epilogue to *Madame Bovary*', *French Studies Bulletin*, 62, Spring 1997.

RAITT, Alan: *Flaubert et le théâtre*, Berne, Peter Lang, 1998.

RAITT, Alan: 'The Strange Case of Emma Bovary's Brother', *French Studies Bulletin*, Spring 1998.

RAITT, Alan: 'Emma Bovary's Pyramid', *French Studies*, January 2001.

RAMAZANI, Vaheed K.: *Flaubert and the Free Indirect Mode*, Charlottesville, University Press of Virginia, 1988.

REY, Pierre-Louis: Madame Bovary *de Gustave Flaubert*, Paris, Folio, 1996.

RICHARD, Jean-Pierre: *Littérature et Sensation. Stendhal, Flaubert*, Paris, Seuil, 1970.

RINEHART, Keith: 'The Structure of *Madame Bovary*', *French Review*, XXI, 1957–1958.

ROUSSET, Jean: *Forme et Signification*, Paris, Corti, 1962.

SACHS, Murray: 'La Fonction du comique dans *Madame Bovary*', *Langages de Flaubert*, ed. M. Issacharoff, Paris, Lettres Modernes, 1976.

SAINTE-BEUVE, Charles-Augustin: '*Madame Bovary*', *Le Moniteur universel*, 4 mai 1857.

SARRAUTE, Nathalie: 'Flaubert le précurseur', *Preuves*, février 1965.

SARTRE, Jean-Paul: *L'Idiot de la famille*, Paris, Gallimard, 1966.

SCHMID, Marion: *Processes of Literary Creation. Flaubert and Proust*, Oxford, Legenda, 1998.

SEEBACHER, Jacques: 'Chiffres, écritures, inscriptions dans *Madame Bovary*', *La Production du sens chez Flaubert*, Paris, UGE, 1975.

SHERRINGTON, R.J.: *Three Novels by Flaubert*, Oxford, Clarendon Press, 1970.

THIBAUDET, Albert: *Gustave Flaubert*, Paris, Gallimard, 1973.

THORLBY, Anthony: *Flaubert and the Art of Realism*, London, Bowes & Bowes, 1956.

TOOKE, Adrianne: *Flaubert and the Pictorial Arts. From Image to Text*, Oxford University Press, 2000.

TRICOTEL, Claude: *Comme Deux Troubadours*, Paris, SEDES, 1978.

WAGNER, Burkhard: *Innenbereich und Äusserung. Flaubertsche Formen indirekter Darstellung and Grundtypen der erlebten Rede*, Munich, Fink, 1972.

WILLIAMS, D.A.: 'Generalisations in *Madame Bovary*', *Neophilologus*, LXII, 1978.

WILLIAMS, D.A.: 'Le Rôle de Binet dans *Madame Bovary*', in *Flaubert, la Dimension du texte*, ed. P.M. Wetherill, Manchester University Press, 1981.

ZENKINE, Serge: Madame Bovary. *L'Oppression réaliste*, Association des Publications de la Faculté des Lettres et Sciences Humaines de Clermont-Ferrand, 1996.

OTHER WORKS MENTIONED

BALZAC, Honoré de: *Le Père Goriot*, ed. Pierre-Georges Castex, Paris, Garnier, 1960.

BALZAC, Honoré de: *L'Œuvre de Balzac*, Paris, Club Français du Livre, 1964.

BALZAC, Honoré de: *Lettres à Madame Hanska*, ed. Roger Pierrot, Paris, Delta, 1969.

BARRERE, Jean-Bertrand: *Hugo, l'Homme et l'Œuvre*, Paris, Boivin, 1952.

BEGUIN, Albert: *Balzac Visionnaire*, Geneva, Skira, 1946.

BELLOS, David: *Balzac Criticism in France 1850–1900*, Oxford, Clarendon Press, 1976.

CHATEAUBRIAND, François-René de: *Œuvres romanesques et voyages*, ed. Maurice Regard, Paris, Bibliothèque de la Pléiade, t.I, 1969.

MERIMEE, Prosper: *Correspondance*, ed. Maurice Parturier, Jean Mallion and Pierre Josserand, Paris, Le Divan / Toulouse, Privat, 1941–1964.

VILLIERS DE L'ISLE-ADAM, *Correspondance générale*, ed. Joseph Bollery, Paris, Mercure de France, 1962.

WRIGHT, Barbara: 'Quinet's *Ahasvérus*, an alternative "drame total"', *French Studies Bulletin*, 5, Winter, 1982–1983.

ZOLA, Emile: *Carnets d'enquête*, ed. Henri Mitterand, Paris, Plon, 1986.

Notes

1   Julian Barnes: 'Justin: A Small Major Character', in *The Process of Art. Studies in Nineteenth-Century Literature and Art presented to Alan Raitt*, ed. Michael Freeman *et al.*, Oxford, Clarendon Press, 1998, p.10. See also Julian Barnes: 'Letter from Genoa', *Times Literary Supplement*, November 26, 1999.

2   Marion Schmid: *Processes of Literary Creation. Flaubert and Proust*, Oxford, Legenda, 1998, p.55.

3   Claude Mouchard and Jacques Neefs: *Flaubert*, Paris, Balland, 1986, pp.373–412.

4   Nathalie Sarraute: 'Flaubert le précurseur', *Preuves*, février 1965.

5   Stephen Heath: *Flaubert: 'Madame Bovary'*, Cambridge University Press, 1992, pp.137–148.

6   Mireille Naturel: *Flaubert et Proust: un secret d'écriture*, Amsterdam / Atlanta, Rodopi, 1999. See also Margaret Mein: 'Flaubert: a Precursor of Proust', *French Studies*, XVII, 1963.

7   The fundamental study of Flaubert before *Madame Bovary* is Jean Bruneau: *Les Débuts littéraires de Gustave Flaubert 1831–1845*, Paris, Colin, 1962. Among other works on partial or analogous subjects one may mention: René Descharmes, *Flaubert, sa vie, son caractère, ses idées avant 1857*, Paris, Ferroud, 1909; Edouard Maynial, *La Jeunesse de Flaubert*, Paris, Mercure de France, 1913; Germaine Mason, *Les Ecrits de jeunesse de Flaubert*, Paris, Gallimard, 1971; René Dumesnil, *La Vocation de Flaubert*, Paris, Gallimard, 1961; E.L. Gans, *The Discovery of Illusion. Flaubert's early works 1835–1837*, Berkeley, University of California Press, 1971.

8   On this question, see Alan Raitt: *Flaubert et le théâtre*, Berne, Peter Lang, 1998.

9   Gustave Flaubert: *Souvenirs, Notes et Pensées intimes*, ed. J. P. Germain, Paris, Nizet, 1987, pp.13–14.

10   See Jean Bruneau: *Les Débuts littéraires...*, pp.53–62.

11   Ibid., pp.122–123.

12   Ibid., p.27.

13   *Corr.* t.I, p.6, to Ernest Chevalier, 4 février 183[2]: 'Je t'avais dit que je ferais des pièces, mais non, je ferai des Romans que j'ai dans la tête, qui sont la belle

Andalouse, le bal masqué, Cadenio, Dorothée la mauresque le curieux impertinent': these are mostly anecdotes taken from *Don Quixote*; p.15, to Chevalier [29 août 1834]: 'J'avance dans mon roman d'Isabeau de Bavière dont j'ai fait le double depuis que je suis revenu de mon voyage de Pont-l'Evêque' – nothing is known of this work, but 'le double' cannot have been very substantial, since Flaubert had only just returned from Pont-l'Evêque a few days earlier.

14 The story is told both by the Goncourts and by Flaubert's niece Caroline (see Raitt: *Flaubert et le théâtre*, pp.24–25).

15 See Raitt: *Flaubert le théâtre*, pp.25–27, and Barbara Wright: 'Quinet's *Ahasvérus*, an alternative "drame total"', *French Studies Bulletin*, 5, Winter, 1982–1983.

16 See Bruneau: *Les Débuts littéraires...*, pp.165–374.

17 Ibid., p.471.

18 Maxime Du Camp: *Souvenirs littéraires*, 3è édition, Paris, Hachette, 1906, t.I, pp.220–221. According to Du Camp, Flaubert's father fell asleep while his son was reading aloud to him something he had written, and on waking said: 'Ecrire est une distraction qui n'est pas mauvaise en soi: cela vaut mieux que d'aller au café ou de perdre son argent au jeu: mais que faut-il pour écrire? Une plume, de l'encre et du papier, rien de plus: n'importe qui, s'il est de loisir, peut faire un roman comme M. Hugo ou M. de Balzac. La littérature, la poésie, à quoi cela sert-il? Nul ne l'a jamais su [...] Le beau métier [...] que de se tremper les doigts dans l'encre! Si je n'avais manié qu'une plume, mes enfants n'auraient pas de quoi vivre aujourd'hui'.

19 The plan of this play was published by Marie-Jeanne Durry: *Flaubert et ses projets inédits*, Paris, Nizet, 1950, pp.119–121.

20 On the question of his work on Voltaire's theatre, see Raitt: *Flaubert et le théâtre*, pp.45–51.

21 *Par les champs et par les grèves*, ed. Adrianne Tooke, Geneva, Droz, 1997.

22 On this and analogous topics, see Adrianne Tooke's admirable *Flaubert and the Pictorial Arts. From Image to Text*, Oxford University Press, 2000.

23 See Jean Bruneau: *Le Conte oriental de Gustave Flaubert*, Paris, Denoel, 1973.

24 Ibid., pp.89–93.

25 Du Camp: *Souvenirs littéraires*, t.I, p.315.

26 Ibid., p.317.

27   Quoted by Jean-Bertrand Barrère: *Hugo, l'homme et l'œuvre*, Paris, Boivin, 1952, p.14.

28   Honoré de Balzac: *Lettres à Madame Hanska*, ed. Roger Pierrot, Paris, Delta, 1969, t.I, p.300.

29   Villiers de l'Isle-Adam: *Correspondance générale*, ed. Joseph Bollery, Paris, Mercure de France, 1962, t.I, p.30.

30   Compare Flaubert: 'Emportez-moi, tempêtes du Nouveau Monde, qui déracinez les arbres séculaires et tourmentez les lacs où les serpents se jouent dans les flots!' (CHH, t.XI, p.664) with this apostrophe from René: 'Orages désirés, levez-vous, qui devez emporter René dans les espaces d'une autre vie' (Chateaubriand, *Œuvres romanesques et Voyages*, ed. Maurice Regard, Paris, Bibliothèque de la Pléiade, t.I, p.1969).

31   In a letter to Sainte-Beuve, Flaubert says of himself: 'moi, qui lisais au Collège *Volupté* et *Les Consolations*' (Corr., II, p.710).

32   Du Camp: *Souvenirs littéraires*, t.I, p.167.

33   Bruneau: *Les Débuts littéraires...*, p.398–400.

34   CHH, t.VIII, pp.13–14. I have corrected Maurice Bardèche's text, where a slip of the pen has substituted Xavier de Ricard for Auguste Ricard.

35   Du Camp: *Souvenirs littéraires*, t.I, p.168.

36   'Quant à Beyle, je n'ai rien compris à l'enthousiasme de Balzac pour un semblable écrivain' (Corr., t.II, p.179).

37   For more detail, see Alan Raitt: 'Le Balzac de Flaubert', *L'Année balzacienne*, 1991.

38   Jean Pommier: '*La Muse du département* et le thème de la femme mal mariée chez Balzac, Mérimée et Flaubert', *L'Année balzacienne*, 1961.

39   Roger Bismut: 'Flaubert et *Le Médecin de campagne* de Balzac', *Les Amis de Flaubert*, mai 1965.

40   Raitt: 'Le Balzac de Flaubert'.

41   Ibid.

42   Jean Pommier et Gabrielle Leleu: Madame Bovary *Nouvelle Version précédée des scénarios inédits*, Paris, Corti, 1949, p.225.

43   Par exemple, Balzac a écrit un jour: 'J'ai conservé *César Birotteau* pendant six ans à l'état d'ébauche, en désespérant de pouvoir jamais intéresser qui que ce soit à la figure d'un boutiquier assez bête, assez médiocre [...] Eh! bien, monsieur, dans un jour de bonheur, je me suis dit: "Il faut le transformer, en en

faisant l'image de la probité! Et il m'a paru possible. Croyez-vous qu'il soit colossal!"' (*L'Œuvre de Balzac*, Paris, Club Français du Livre, t.14, p.1222).

44   *Madame Bovary*, CHH, t.I, p.481.

45   Quoted in Gustave Flaubert: *Pour Louis Bouilhet*, ed. Alan Raitt, Exeter University Press, 1994, p.50.

46   Quoted in Du Camp: *Souvenirs littéraires*, t.II, p.153.

47   Quoted in *Madame Bovary*, ed. René Dumesnil, Paris, Les Belles Lettres, 1945, p.CL.

48   Quoted in Claude Tricotel: *Comme Deux Troubadours*, Paris, SEDES, 1978, p.21.

49   Quoted in *Madame Bovary*, ed. Paul Vernière, Paris, Éditions de Cluny, 1951, p.435.

50   Ibid., p.386.

51   Du Camp, *Souvenirs littéraires*, t.II, p.150.

52   Quoted by Pierre-Louis Rey: Madame Bovary *de Gustave Flaubert*, Paris, Folio, 1996, pp.158–160.

53   Quoted in *Madame Bovary*, ed. Jacques Neefs, Livre de Poche classique, 1999, p.544.

54   Quoted in René Descharmes et René Dumesnil: *Autour de Flaubert*, Paris, Mercure de France, 1912, t.I, p.71.

55   Quoted by René Descharmes and René Dumesnil: *Autour de Flaubert*, t.I, p.83.

56   Among studies on this subject, one may mention Marianne Bonwit: *Gustave Flaubert et le Principe d'impassibilité*, Berkeley and Los Angeles, University of California Publications in Modern Philology, vol.33, University of California Press, 1950.

57   Bruneau, *Les Débuts littéraires...*, p.557.

58   See Victor Brombert: 'La première *Education sentimentale*: roman de l'artiste', *Europe*, septembre–octobre–novembre 1969.

59   Edmond and Jules de Goncourt: *Journal*, ed. Robert Ricatte, Paris, Fasquelle–Flammarion, 1956, t.II, p.903.

60   D. A. Williams: 'Generalisations in *Madame Bovary*', *Neophilologus*, LXII, 1978.

61   For instance, of Charles's mother: 'Alors elle s'était tue, avalant sa rage dans un stoïcisme muet, qu'elle garda jusqu'à sa mort' (p.54); in fact, she only dies on the last page of the book.

62   Albert Thibaudet (*Gustave Flaubert*, Paris, Gallimard, 1973, p.228) wonders if this metaphor is not 'la plus longue et la plus laborieuse de toute la littérature française'.

63   Don Demorest: *L'Expression figurée et symbolique dans l'œuvre de Gustave Flaubert*, Geneva, Slatkine Reprints, 1967, p.420.

64   Ibid., p.424.

65   For instance Léon Bopp: *Commentaire sur* Madame Bovary, Neuchâtel, La Baconnière, 1951, p.123: 'Comparé à d'autres descriptions de Flaubert intimement liées au mouvement du récit, entraînées par lui, ce tableau a paru, long, compact, trop détaché de la narration, et aussi morne qu'une page de Baedeker'.

66   Henry James: 'Gustave Flaubert' in *Selected Criticism*. ed. M. Shapira, London, Heinemann, 1968, p.222.

67   Indeed, Minnelli seems to have set out to make Charles more sympathetic, since in the film he draws back from performing the operation on Hippolyte for fear of making a mistake.

68   R.J. Sherrington: *Three Novels by Flaubert*, Oxford, Clarendon Press, 1970, pp.92–93. See also Graham Falconer: 'Flaubert assassin de Charles', *Langages de Flaubert*, ed. M. Issacharoff, Paris, Lettres Modernes, 1976.

69   There are several excellent and detailed analyses of dialogue and 'style indirect libre' in Flaubert's novels: Burkhard Wagner: *Innenbereich and Äusserung. Flaubertsche Formen indirekter Darstellung und Grundtypen der erlebten Rede*, Munich, Fink, 1972; Stirling Haig: *Flaubert and the Gift of Speech, Dialogue and Discourse in four 'modern' novels*, Cambridge University Press, 1986; Marie-Thérèse Mathet: *Le Dialogue romanesque chez Flaubert*, Paris, Aux Amateurs de livres, 1988; Vaheed K. Ramazani: *Flaubert and the free indirect Mode*, Charlottesville, University Press of Virginia, 1988.

70   Du Camp: *Souvenirs littéraires*, t.I, p.164.

71   See Raitt: *Flaubert et le théâtre*, pp.36–37 and 150–151.

72   Claudine Gothot-Mersch: 'De *Madame Bovary* à *Bouvard et Pécuchet*: la parole des personnages dans les romans de Flaubert', *Revue d'Histoire littéraire de la France*, juillet–octobre 1981.

73   Ibid.

74   Ibid.

75   Haig: *Flaubert and the Gift of Speech...*, p.41.

76   Claude Duchet: 'Discours social et texte italique dans *Madame Bovary*', *Langages de Flaubert*.

77   George Pistorius: '*La Structure des comparaisons dans* Madame Bovary', *Cahiers de l'Association Internationale des Etudes françaises*, 1971.

78   Mathet: *Le Dialogue romanesque...*, pp.248–250.

79   Ibid., p.247.

80   Haig: *Flaubert and the Gift of Speech...*, p.172.

81   Studies of description in Flaubert include Antoine-Youssef Naaman: *Les Débuts de Gustave Flaubert et sa technique de la description*, Paris, Nizet, 1962; Benjamin F. Bart: *Flaubert's Landscape Descriptions*, Ann Arbor, University of Michigan Press, 1956; Geneviève Bollème: *La Leçon de Flaubert*, Paris, Julliard, 1964.

82   Quoted in *Madame Bovary*, ed. Jacques Neefs, p.544.

83   Quoted in Descharmes and Dumesnil: *Autour de Flaubert*, t.I, p.74.

84   Honoré de Balzac: *Le Père Goriot*, ed. Pierre-Georges Castex, Paris, Garnier, 1960, p.13.

85   Edmond and Jules de Goncourt: *Journal*, t.I, p.888–889.

86   Claudine Gothot-Mersch: *La Genèse de* Madame Bovary, Paris, Corti, 1966, p.99–100.

87   Bollème: *La Leçon...*, p.136.

88   Pommier and Leleu: *Nouvelle Version...*, pp.200–201.

89   Bollème: *La Leçon...*, p.195.

90   Prosper Mérimée: *Correspondance*, ed. Maurice Parturier, Jean Mallion and Pierre Josserand, Paris, Le Divan / Toulouse, Privat, 1941–1964, t.XI, pp.250–251.

91   Ibid., t.XIV, p.686.

92   Works dealing with Flaubert's relations with Realism include Anthony Thorlby: *Flaubert: the Art of Realism*, London, Bowes & Bowes, 1956; and Serge Zenkine: Madame Bovary: *l'Oppression réaliste*, Clermont-Ferrand, Association des Publications de la Faculté des Lettres et Sciences humaines de Clermont-Ferrand, 1996.

93   Jean Bruneau: 'La Famille Collier et Flaubert', *Nineteenth-Century French Studies*, Fall–Winter 1988–1989.

94   Quoted in *Madame Bovary*, ed. Paul Vernière, p.387.

95   Quoted in David Bellos: *Balzac Criticism in France 1850–1900*, Oxford, Clarendon Press, 1976, p.141.

96   Félicien Marceau: introduction to *Madame Bovary*, Paris, Livre de poche, 1961.

97   Alberto Cento: *Il Realismo documentario nell'*Education sentimentale, Naples, Liguori, 1967.

98   Emile Zola: *Carnets d'enquête*, ed. Henri Mitterand, Paris, Plon, 1986.

99   Guy de Maupassant: *Pour Gustave Flaubert*, Bruxelles, Complexe, 1986, p.27.

100 Ibid., p.51.

101 Ibid., p.51.

102 The most thorough exploration of Flaubert's style is Don Demorest: *L'Expression figurée....* But one may also consult two other studies – Anna Ahlström: *Etude sur la langue de Flaubert*, Macon, Privat, 1900, and Paul Binswanger, *Die ästhetische Problematik Flauberts; Untersuchungen zum Problem von Sprache und Stil in der Literatur*, Frankfurt, Klostermann, 1934.

103 Marcel Proust: *Sur Baudelaire, Flaubert et Morand*, Bruxelles, Complexe, 1987, p.63.

104 Ibid., p.69.

105 Roger Huss: 'Some anomalous Uses of the Imperfect and the Status of Action in Flaubert', *French Studies*, XXXI, 1977.

106 Gérard Genette: 'Silences de Flaubert', in *Figures*, Paris, Seuil, 1966, p.237.

107 Ibid., p.239.

108 Ibid., p.239.

109 See p.80.

110 Genette: *Figures*, p.243.

111 Proust: *Sur Baudelaire...*, pp.71–72.

112 Huss: 'Some anomalous Uses...'.

113 Pommier and Leleu: *Nouvelle Version...*, p.150.

114 Ibid., p.134.

115 Proust: *Sur Baudelaire...*, p.65.

116 Albert Béguin: *Balzac visionnaire*, Geneva, Skira, 1946, p.21.

117 See Joelle Gleize: 'Le Défaut de ligne droite', *Littérature*, octobre, 1974.

118 Murray Sachs: 'La Fonction du comique dans *Madame Bovary*', *Langages de Flaubert*.

119 Michel Crouzet: 'Le Style épique dans *Madame Bovary*', *Europe*, septembre–octobre–novembre 1969.

120 Demorest: *L'Expression figurée...*, p.420.

121 Ibid., p.476.

122 Proust: *Sur Baudelaire...*, p.64.

123 Ibid., p.64.

124 See pp.141–142 for another interpretation.

125 Thibaudet (*Flaubert*, p.272) notes that the expression occurs in direct speech with Homais employing it. So the grammatical irregularity is a perfectly acceptable representation of colloquial usage.

126 Ibid., p.249.

127 Ibid., p.244.

128 Quoted by Jean-Pierre Richard: *Littérature et Sensation. Stendhal, Flaubert*, Paris, Seuil, 1970, p.237.

129 Jean Rousset: *Forme et Signification*, Paris, Corti, 1962, p.133.

130 Gothot-Mersch: *La Genèse...*, p.238.

131 Germaine Mason: 'Les Deux Clairs de lune dans *Madame Bovary*', *French Studies*, July 1954.

132 Jean Pommier: 'Noms et Prénoms dans *Madame Bovary*. Essai d'ono-mastique littéraire', in *Dialogues avec le passé*, Paris, Nizet, 1976.

133 Margaret Lowe: *Towards the Real Flaubert: a Study of* Madame Bovary, Oxford, Clarendon Press, 1984, pp.64–84.

134 D. A. Williams: 'Le Rôle de Binet dans *Madame Bovary*', in *Flaubert: la Dimension du texte*, ed. P. M. Wetherill, Manchester University Press, 1982.

135 This chapter largely reproduces my article 'Emma Bovary's Pyramid', *French Studies*, January 2001, and I am grateful to the Editorial Board for permission to use it.

136 Descharmes and Dumesnil: *Autour de Flaubert*, t.II, p.48.

137 Jean-Pierre Duquette: *Flaubert ou l'architecture du vide*, Presses de l'Université de Montréal, 1972, p.130.

138 Pierre-Louis Rey: *'Madame Bovary'...*, pp.146–147.

139 Keith Rinehart: 'The Structure of *Madame Bovary*', *French Review*, XXI, 1957–1958.

140 Alison Fairlie: *Flaubert: Madame Bovary*, London, Arnold, 1962, p.30.

141 Gothot-Mersch: *La Genèse...*, p.238.

142 Rey: *'Madame Bovary...'*, p.54. See also Jacques Seebacher: 'Chiffres, écritures, inscriptions dans *Madame Bovary*' in *La Production du sens chez Flaubert*, Paris, U.G.E., 1975; and Roger Bismut: 'Sur une chronologie de *Madame Bovary*', *Les Amis de Flaubert*, mai 1953.

143 This may be compared with the German novel most closely related to *Madame Bovary*, Theodor Fontane's *Effi Briest*, the title of which is the heroine's maiden name.

144 Diverse: *Autour d'Emma: Madame Bovary un film de Claude Chabrol avec Isabelle Huppert*, Paris, Hatier, 1991, p.55. In answer to a question by Pierre-Marc de Biasi about his choice of an elliptical ending for the film, Chabrol replied: 'D'abord, j'avais à choisir entre l'hypothèse de mettre en scène la mort de Charles et celle de la mentionner comme je l'ai finalement fait... J'ai décidé de ne pas la mettre en scène, tout comme j'ai décidé aussi de me priver de la rencontre finale entre Rodolphe et Charles. C'étaient pourtant des moments formidables pour un metteur en scène. Vous savez, il en coûte de faire des ellipses! Mais j'avais de bonnes raisons de procéder comme cela. D'abord, comme je vous l'ai dit, il y a le fait que cette histoire est celle d'Emma, et qu'après sa disparition de l'écran, il devient très difficile de soutenir l'attention du spectateur sur autre chose: là aussi, la poétique du récit n'est pas la même dans un livre et dans un film. Quand le héros disparaît définitivement du film, il faut conclure très vite: des développements narratifs après cela deviennent insupportables même s'ils sont parfaits: l'émotion n'y est plus. C'est comme cela'.

145 Rey: *Madame Bovary...*, pp.145–146.

146 Margaret Lowe: *Towards the real Flaubert...*, pp.64–84.

147 Jeanne Bem: *Clefs pour L'Education sentimentale*, Tübingen, Narr / Paris, Place, 1981, p.64.

148 Gothot-Mersch: *La Genèse...*, pp.290–291.

149 For a reading of *Madame Bovary* which strongly contests the traditional view of it, see Jonathan Culler: *Flaubert: the Uses of Uncertainty*, London, Elek, 1974.

150 Stratton Buck: 'The Chronology of the *Education sentimentale*', *Modern Language Notes*, February 1952; and Joseph Pinatel: 'Notes vétilleuses sur la chronologie de *L'Education sentimentale*', *Revue d'Histoire littéraire de la France*, janvier–mars, 1953.

151 Alan Raitt: 'The Strange Case of Emma Bovary's Brother', *French Studies Bulletin*, Spring 1998.

152 Ibid.

153 See *Madame Bovary*, ed. Gothot-Mersch, p.452, n.3.

154 Reproduced in Thibaudet, *Flaubert*, (Documents).

155 Pommier and Leleu, *Nouvelle Version...*, p.22.

156 Ibid., p.142.

157 Claudine Gothot-Mersch: 'Le Point de vue dans *Madame Bovary*', *Cahiers de l'Association Internationale des Etudes françaises*, 1971.

158 See Alan Raitt: 'Nous étions à l'étude...', in *Gustave Flaubert II*, Paris, Lettres Modernes, 1986.

159 Gérard Genette: *Figures III*, Paris, Seuil, 1972, p.253.

160 Quoted in *Madame Bovary*, ed. Vernière, p.370.

161 Pommier and Leleu: *Nouvelle Version...*, p.129, and Yvan Leclerc, *Plans et Scénarios de* Madame Bovary, Paris, Editions du CNRS, Zulma, 1995, p.61.

162 'Paltaquot' is what Flaubert has written, but that must be a slip of the pen for 'paltoquet'.

163 Pommier and Leleu: *Nouvelle Version...*, p.118; Leclerc: *Plans et Scénarios*, p.58.

164 Alan Raitt: 'The Date of the projected Epilogue to *Madame Bovary*', *French Studies Bulletin*, 62, Spring, 1997.

165 Jean-Paul Sartre: *L'Idiot de la famille*, Paris, Gallimard, 1966, p.8.

166 Bernard Masson, in *Gustave Flaubert I: Flaubert et après*, Paris, Lettres Modernes, 1984, p.4.

Index

Le Romantisme et après en France
Romanticism and after in France

edited by Alan Raitt

"Le Romantisme et après en France" est une nouvelle collection dont le but est de publier des monographies ou des ouvrages de plus longue haleine, écrits par des membres des universités du Royaume-Uni et d'Irlande, que ce soit des enseignants chevronnés ou de jeunes chercheurs. Ces livres traiteront de la littérature française depuis la période préromantique jusqu'aux premières années du vingtième siècle, et pourront être en anglais ou en français; ils pourront traiter d'un seul auteur ou d'un sujet plus étendu.

"Romanticism and after in France" is a new series designed to publish monographs or longer works of high quality originating in universities in the United Kingdom and Ireland, whether by established scholars or recent graduates, dealing with French literature in the period from pre-Romanticism to the turn of the twentieth century. Books may be in English or French, and may consist of studies of single authors or of wider topics.